Teaching Consultation Process SOURCEBOOK

Susan Edington & Cathy Hunt

NEW FORUMS PRESS INC.
Stillwater, Oklahoma

Table of Contents

Acknowledgement

We gratefully acknowledge the work and support of two people who made possible this Sourcebook—Judy Rhoads and Mike Kerwin. Not only was the Sourcebook Judy's idea, she also wrote the Summer Fellowship Proposals which made it possible to begin this project. Mike Kerwin is the University of Kentucky Community College System's Teaching Consultation Process expert. His pioneering work at UK, expertise, and support made it possible to complete this project. We also wish to acknowledge Sheila Foreman who typed, proofed, and retyped this manuscript. Her cheerful work on this project far exceeded her job description. Thank you, Judy, Mike, and Sheila!

Susan Edington and Cathy Hunt

Introduction

The University of Kentucky Community College System Sourcebook for the Teaching Consultation Program was developed to help teaching consultants assist their colleagues in making changes in their teaching behavior. More specifically, it was developed as a resource that teaching consultants could use in the planning and implementation phase of the Teaching Consultation Program. A brief introduction to this program, therefore, should help the reader to make more effective use of the Sourcebook.

The Teaching Consultation Program, implemented in 1977, and originally called the Teaching Improvement Process, has been one of the effective and popular faculty development programs offered in the University of Kentucky Community College System. Each of the 14 colleges that comprise the System offers the program, and over 800 faculty have participated in it. Participants have consistently given the program high ratings.

Basically, TCP provides a consulting service to faculty who want to analyze their teaching and implement changes. Faculty members who are recognized by their colleagues as outstanding teachers and have attended a Teaching Consultants' Workshop serve as consultants. Teaching consultants work with two instructors each semester and are released from one 3-hour class to do so. In the 1993 fall semester, 24 consultants worked with 48 faculty in 13 of the 14 UKCCS campuses.

Using TCP, consultants follow a set of procedures originally developed at the School of Education of the University of Massachusetts at Amherst. Teaching consultants in UKCCS have revised these procedures somewhat, however, to more effectively meet the needs of faculty teaching in the community college setting. The procedures are designed to help faculty recognize and develop instructional behaviors most appropriate for themselves and their students and are organized into five stages. These five stages are outlined below.

1. *Initial Interview.* The consultant meets with the faculty member, clarifies the confidential nature of their relationship, explains the process, and identifies a specific class on which to concentrate. The consultant asks the faculty member to agree to participate in the program for the entire semester. If the faculty member agrees to participate, the consultant arranges to begin collecting the data.

2. *Data Collection.* The consultant interviews the faculty member, observes him or her teaching the class, videotapes an instructional session, and administers a questionnaire to the students in the class to obtain information about the instructor's goals and teaching behaviors. This stage requires about four weeks.

3. *Data Review and Analysis.* The consultant and the faculty member review the collected data. Together they identify at least three teaching behaviors that both believe to be strengths and three teaching behaviors that both believe should be changed.

4. *Planning and Implementing Changes.* The consultant and the faculty member identify three or four changes that they would like to make in the class. The consultant helps the faculty member to select or design and implement strategies to make these changes. This stage requires at least eight weeks and the consultant monitors the instructor's progress weekly.

5. *Evaluation.* In the final three weeks of the semester, the consultant evaluates the instructor's success in achieving his or her goals. To accomplish this, another classroom visitation is made, another class is videotaped, and another questionnaire is administered to students. The data is reviewed by the consultant and the instructor, and the instructor evaluates his or her experience in the program.

One of the key components of TCP is the Teaching Analysis by Students (TABS) questionnaire that is used in the data collection stage. Based upon extensive research by Robert Wilson and others at the University of California at Berkeley, this questionnaire was developed originally at the University of Massachusetts at Amherst. The original questionnaire contained 38 items describing instructional behaviors and 12 items describing student characteristics. Although the questionnaire used in TCP contains 50 items, many of the items have been reworded or changed to make the questionnaire more descriptive and on a lower reading level.

Although consultants follow a well-defined set of procedures in TCP and use a research-based student questionnaire as a part of the data collection process, the crucial element in the program is the consultant's ability to assist his or her colleagues in recognizing and consciously developing instructional behaviors most appropriate for themselves and their students. The Teaching Consultant Program itself assists the consultant in this process by being organized around 18 groups of behaviors that research on teaching and the experience of the consultants have shown to be important to faculty and students. These groups of behaviors are identified and defined below.

Logical Organization. Logical organization refers to the instructor's ability to design in-class instruction to facilitate learning. This includes the organization of course materials and learning activities to facilitate learning for the student.

Variety of Instructional Resources. Variety of instructional resources refers to the instructor's ability to use and design effective instructional resources to support teacher objectives and student needs.

Motivation. The instructor's skill in creating the forces to elicit and continue the student's desire to learn.

Communication Skills. The instructor's ability to use effective verbal and nonverbal behaviors at a pace which enhances student learning.

Variety of Methods. The instructor's ability to select and design teaching methods to achieve student objectives.

Application and Integration. The instructor's ability to help students develop critical thinking skills for integrating information for application in and out of the classroom.

Classroom Evaluation and Assessment. The instructor's ability to evaluate and measure student performance.

Interpersonal Relations. The instructor's ability to be available to students and relate to students in a way which promotes mutual respect.

Classroom Management. The instructor's skill in performing organizational and administrative tasks that allow instructor to proceed smoothly and efficiently.

Student Diversity. The instructor's ability to recognize and attend to the differing ability, learning style, culture, age, gender, and interests of students.

Learning Environment. The instructor's ability to create an appropriate physical, social, and intellectual environment for maximum student learning.

Value Context. The instructor's skill in assisting students in the exploration of their own values and in realizing the implications of those values for their professional and private conduct.

Enthusiasm. The instructor's ability to convey to students a strong interest in course content and in the students themselves.

Classroom Discussion. The instructor's skill in facilitating student involvement in class discussion and in group work or activities.

Asking and Responding to Questions. The instructor's ability to use appropriate questions for instructional purposes and to answer questions clearly to promote understanding and participation.

Establishing a Learning Set. The instructor's ability to clarify, communicate, and arouse interest in learning objectives.

Creativity. The instructor's incorporation of opportunities for divergent thinking in solving problems and recognition of creative thought in the classroom.

Closure. The instructor's ability to provide a summary experience for the integration of major points at the end of an objective and at the conclusion of a class session.

Delineating these 18 groups of behaviors does not imply that other variables of the teaching and learning situation are not important. Consultants recognize that such things as entering behavior, motivation of students, prior knowledge, the intellectual climate of the institution, the nature and the pacing of student rewards, the various learning styles represented by the students in the class and the subject matter itself, and the physical characteristics of the classroom interact continuously to affect the quality of education and learning produced by students. Whereas many of these variables cannot be controlled, however, others can. TCP focuses on behaviors that can be changed by the instructor.

The 18 groups of behaviors identified above are not intended to be inclusive of all of the behaviors that can be changed by the instructor. They simply serve as a framework for the program and as springboards for thinking about change. Giving an illustration of how they are used may be helpful.

The teaching behaviors are introduced to the faculty member in one of the initial consultation sessions. Together, the consultant and faculty member review the individual behaviors and definitions to create a frame of reference for discussion throughout the consultation process. The faculty member is made aware of the Sourcebook, which contains a chapter on each of the behaviors. The faculty member has access to the Sourcebook throughout the consultation process.

After the initial data gathering, which includes the interview, classroom materials, classroom observation, videotape, and student questionnaire (TABS), the consultant and faculty member work together to identify strengths of the faculty member and opportunities for growth and improvement. For instance, the data collected might indicate that the faculty member: (1) showed respect for students; (2) was enthusiastic; (3) spoke clearly; and, (4) related the course to everyday life. On the other hand, the data showed that the faculty member could improve in the following areas: (1) identifying major and minor points; (2) using a variety of methods and materials; and, (3) improving the opening and closing of the class session.

The background information on the student questionnaire has data concerning students in the class; their attitudes toward the subject matter and the instructor and how they feel about the difficulty of the class, the level of structure, and goals of the instructor. Using all this information together with the strengths and opportunities for improvement, the consultant and faculty member set long- and short-term goals for improving instruction.

In this case, the instructor might set goals in the areas of student participation and involving students through active learning strategies, which might include Dyad groups, the 1-minute paper, case studies, and/or role plays. Goals may include moving around more while lecturing and further enhancing communication skills which might set the stage for student involvement. Again, the behaviors are used as starting points for discussion and development of the goals.

The teaching skills approach has several advantages over more global approaches.

1. It is flexible; the skills can be combined and weighed in different proportions, depending on the faculty member and his/her teaching area.
2. A strong teaching skills base provides flexibility for the instructor in meeting the changing needs of the student population and in exploring a variety of different teaching methods.
3. The 18 skills are applicable to most instructional situations, although for one instructor, some behaviors may assume more importance than for another instructor. The teaching consultation process, using the behaviors, has been utilized in Kentucky for 18 years with laboratories, traditional classrooms, team-teaching, and with high school teachers.

The skills were extracted from a review of: (1) a revised version of TABS as used by Kentucky consultants; (2) published literature in the field of teaching; (3) inductive studies of effective teaching; and, (4) research in the area of higher education. The 18 are not exhaustive or comprehensive in nature. The behaviors reflect an active approach to learning by students and reflect the language and direction for teaching as shown in the literature.

The Sourcebook contains a chapter on each of the teaching skills as outlined by the teaching consultants. The aim of each chapter is to provide definitions of each behavior, an overview of information available, and current literature on that topic, as well as ideas for strategies to help faculty members improve their instruction with a particular behavior. The references listed at the end of each chapter provide a source for further and more exhaustive exploration of each behavior.

Logical Organization

Logical organization refers to the instructor's ability to design in-class instruction to facilitate learning. This includes the organization of course material and learning activities and/or materials to facilitate learning for the student.

Logical Organization of the Course

To design instruction to facilitate learning, the instructor must deal with the issue of what is to be covered by the course of instruction. Marton (1989) identified three kinds of competence arranged in a taxonomy which colleges should aim to develop: Conceptions, how students perceive and understand important phenomena in the discipline; Skills, what students can do; and, Knowledge, the factual knowledge students possess.

In planning a course, then, the instructor along with other faculty in that discipline, should first ask themselves "What are the most important concepts?" Kember (1991) believes the course would then be sequenced to focus first on the most important concepts and concentrate on ensuring mastery.

Next, instructors need to ask themselves the important question of "What skills do my students need to learn to do?" Probably learning how to access information is an important skill for most disciplines. The details of how, when, and where can be answered later. Last, instructors need to identify the factual knowledge that is important to the understanding of the concepts. Because knowledge is so transient, it is the least important on the taxonomy. In many disciplines the information base is growing rapidly, but its "shelf life," or relevance to the total picture, is diminishing. As a result, students need the skills of their disciplines so they can access the factual knowledge themselves.

Once we determine what we want our students to know and be able to do, we must choose readings and activities to enable them to *excel* in those tasks. That statement implies two important points for course design:

1. We don't have to cover the entire text, and,
2. We *plan* for student success.

Good grades become part of our plan.

"Will this be on the exam?" indicates our students' task-specific approach to learning. If we say "yes," they will study; if we say "no," their eyes glaze over and they stop taking notes. If we say "Know everything we have studied," they cannot separate major points and minor points. The answer to the dilemma, then, is to take advantage of their way of learning by establishing clearly defined objectives for the course, planning readings and activities to accomplish the objectives, and designing tests, quizzes, reports, and projects that *define in operational terms* the overall objectives for the course. Now students won't have to ask if it will be on the exam; they will know by reading the objectives exactly what is expected of them, and they will know that their authentic test will provide meaningful "evidence of knowing" (Wiggins, 1989, p. 705). Students have the right to expect genuine congruence between a course's objectives and the assignments they are asked to complete.

McClymer and Ziegler (1991) report their experience of reinventing an introductory history survey course. After going through the process previously prescribed, they discovered they had already surrendered control of their course content because they had organized their syllabus around a textbook. Regaining control meant they had to "adopt a critical, even adversarial approach to texts" (p. 27). An example of McClymer's and Ziegler's authentic test is this essay question: "Evaluate the career of either Queen Elizabeth I of England or King Henry IV of France in terms of how well her/his key decisions conformed to Machiavelli's advice in *The Prince*" (p. 30). They hand out the essay question *before* beginning to cover the material it was based upon. Next, they share their rationale— "assignment is intended to help you analyze these quite complex and frequently contradictory developments by looking at how a single monarch sought to impose her/his will upon the events of the late sixteenth century. We are not seeking a simple summary of her/his actions" (p. 20). Students understand the rationale of the assignment as well as the requirements for success.

Logical Organization of the Class

A logical organization of a class follows the logical organization of any process. It has a beginning, a middle, and an end. A teacher's class organization corresponds to the advice given to speakers—tell them what you *plan* to tell them, tell them, and then tell them what you told them. This is best accomplished by preparing a lesson plan. See attached.

The following plan is based upon a 50-minute class:

1. Beginning

The class objectives should already be on the board, the assignment should be on the board, and at least a 5-minute "small talk" period should have occurred. Begin class promptly, and use an attention getter. (See chapter on Student Motivation for ideas.) The attention getter serves two purposes: to *engage* students' attention and to provide a stress-free atmosphere conducive for learning. Spend a minimum of five minutes reviewing the last class and then lead into an advance organizer—a way to relate last class's concepts to today's class concept. (See chapter on Establishing a Learning Set.)

2. Middle (30 minutes; 20-minute presentation, 10-minute reinforcement)

After a correlation has been established between what has been learned and what is to be learned, present the new concept. Kember (1991) found that merely presenting a concept is insufficient if genuine understanding is desired. For instance, rather than summarizing material about the behavior of electrons, the teacher could divide the class into small groups of four or five and give each group the following question: "You are an electron in the middle of a copper wire. At a certain time, I will connect a battery across your wire. How will you react before and after connection?" (Bowden, 1988, p. 262). Next, each group would devise a response. The responses would be written on a transparency so the entire class would be able to see everyone's responses. Below is an example of how some participants responded to this activity:

a. My neighbor bumps me immediately and then I bump the neighbor on the other side.
b. I sit still before connection but gradually move together with the others after connection.
c. I gradually accelerate.
d. I take off with the speed of light.
e. Before connection, I am dancing around randomly. I do not feel the field from the battery immediately, but when it gets here (at the speed of light) my dance is biased a bit in the direction of the field (Bowden, 1988, p. 262).

Assuming incorrect conceptions have been revealed in the responses, it is necessary to provide a challenge and feedback to the class. Simply giving the correct answer is not likely to change a group's conception. Feedback should aim to expose the incongruity of the existing misconceptions. Real world examples and counter-examples following from the scenario established in the original question are likely to be effective (Kember, 1991). After misconceptions have been identified, reinforce the correct concept by having groups prepare a visual representation of their understanding. For example, they could draw a diagram, they could make an analogy between the concept and some everyday object or activity and draw that, or they could even role play the concept, assuming the roles of battery, electrons, wire. The important idea is to reinforce the material no matter how you choose to do so. (See chapter on Variety of Methods and Variety of Materials.)

3. End (10 minutes)

The end of class is the last five minutes or so called closure. This is your opportunity to discover how effective the lesson has been and if the objectives established for the class have been met. There are many ways to initiate closure. (See chapter on Closure.) If your teaching style is more traditional, you may simply summarize the lesson; better yet, your students can summarize. A variation might include requesting a 1-minute summary from each student. Another useful technique includes having each student write two possible short answer test questions based on the day's lesson, exchange these with a neighbor, and answer them. The students would grade their neighbor's papers and then pass them in so you could assess their understanding.

Logical organization of the course and class requires reflection, planning, and time; however, the rewards are gratifying as the teacher's self-confidence increases, students' understanding of concepts increases, and students' assessment and evaluation performance increases.

1. *Establishing a Learning Set*—The instructor's ability to clarify, communicate, and arouse interest in the learning objectives.
    a. *Attention Getter*—an item of trivia, a current event, or a word plexer (mce, mce, mce=three blind mice) are ways to get students' attention and to start everyone off smiling. Give a piece of hard candy for answering correctly a plexer and students will be early to class!
    b. *Review of Lesson*—the instructor can review, a student can review, or the instructor can designate someone in each class to take "minutes." The minutes can then be read at the beginning of class. This teaches your students how to summarize and also serves to review the previous class for everyone.
    c. *Overview of Lesson*—I write the day's objectives on the board. As I read them to the students, they know what will happen during the class period and what I hope to accomplish. Other ideas include placing an outline on the overhead, writing questions on the board that students will be able to answer by the end of the period, and asking students to predict in a sentence or two what they should logically expect today's lesson to cover based on yesterday's.
2. *Develop the Lesson*
    a. *Motivation*—there are other ways to motivate students besides saying "This will be on the test"! Ideas include the

LESSON PLAN

KNOWLEDGE:
List
Describe
Define
Label
Name
Fill in
Identify
What
When
Who

COMPREHENSION:
Paraphrase
Explain
Review
Match
Discuss
Translate
Interpret
How
Why

APPLICATION:
Apply
Construct
Draw
Simulate
Sketch
Employ
Restructure
Make
Write
Predict
How
Produce

ANALYSIS:
Classify
Dissect
Distinguish
Differentiate
Compare
Contrast
Categorize
Separate
Break Down
Subdivide

SYNTHESIS:
Combine
Relate
Put Together
Integrate
Assemble
Collect
Produce Original
Find New Combination

EVALUATION:
Judge
Argue
Assess
Appraise
Decide
Defend
Rate
Debate
Evaluate
Choose
Should

Date:_____

Objective: The student will be able to

Procedure:

1. Establish Learning Set.

   A.   Attention Getter

   B.   Review of Previous Lesson

   C.   Overview of Lesson

   D.   Focus

2. Develop Lesson.

   A.   Motivation

   B.   Procedure

   C.   Guided Practice

   D.   Independent Practice

3. Closure.

Evaluation:

Materials Needed:

Tips
1. Wait 3 to 5 sec. for student response to question
2. Use variety of materials
3. Maintain momentum of class
4. Let students do as much of the work and talking as possible
5. Exercise withitness—be alert to boredom, student monopolizers, uncomfortable room temp, messy blackboard, etc.
6. Designate a student to alert you to the last 8 mins. of class for closure
7. Prepare questions in advance, use variety of questions
8. Be early to class, start class on time, be available after class for help
9. Move around the classroom
10. Know everyone's name and use frequently!
11. Foster risk-free learning environment
12. Recognize and cater to different learning styles
13. The first day of class sets the tone and expectations for the rest of the semester
14. Always return tests promptly and go over it with students
15. Consider collaborative tests—or at least a portion—25% collaborative is about right
16. Use some essay tests and short essay tests. The key is careful writing, careful point distribution, and carefully written answer key.
17. Establish a circle drawn on the blackboard for the "parking lot." This is where you can write ideas or discussion topics that are interesting but divergent and time consuming for the moment.

Figure 1

following: 1) Having students estimate the number of yards of carpet needed to carpet the classroom floor and then showing them how to figure area followed by the actual measurement to answer the original question. This real-life application piques students' interest because they see relevance to their lives; too, the instructor has created disequilibrium. 2) Creating disequilibrium—anytime you give students a problem to solve, a riddle or a mystery to uncover, they are motivated by the desire to satisfy their curiosity. 3) Role Playing—students or the instructor can role play. Having the instructor assume the role of Piaget, for instance, to explain cognitive development is more interesting than having the regular instructor!

   b. *Procedure*—there are dozens of ways to proceed. Lecture is still the most common route; however, other ideas include cooperative groups (jigsaw; think, pair, share; structured controversy); simulations such as role play, games, case studies. 4) Mini presentations, clustering, projects, and discussion are also popular methods.

3. *Closure*—This is the instructor's ability to provide a summary experience for the integration of major points at the end of an objective and at the conclusion of a class session.

Ideas for closure include writing one-minute papers, answering the questions the instructor had placed on the board at the beginning of class, having student provide a summary sentence for each objective listed on the board, giving students a concept map to fill in, or reading the class minutes.

4. *Evaluation*—Instructors must determine if identified objectives have been met.

Evaluation does not have to take the form of a test or a quiz, although certainly those are two ways. Formative assessment techniques include quick answer cards, observation, demonstration, one-minute papers, team review, and construction of possible test questions.

References

Bowden, J. (1988). Achieving change in teaching practices. In P. Ramsden (Ed.), *Improving Learning*. London: Kogan Page.

Clymer, J., and Ziegler, P. (1991). The assignment driven course: A task specific approach to teaching. *Journal of Excellence in College Teaching, 2,* 25-33.

Kember, D. (1991). Instructional design for meaningful learning. *Instructional Science, 20,* 289-310.

Marton, F. (1989). Some reflections on the improvement of learning. In J. A. Bowden (Ed.), *Student learning: Research into practice.* Melbourne: Melbourne University Press.

Wiggins, G. (1989). A true test: Toward more authentic and equitable assessment. *Phi Delta Kappan, 70,* 703-713.

Suggested Reading

Baird, J. R. (1988). Quality. What should make higher education "higher?" *Higher Education Research and Development, 7*(2), 141-152.

Baird, J. R., and Mitchell, I. J. (Eds.).(1986). *Improving the quality of teaching and learning: An australian case study—the PEEL Project.* Melbourne: Monash University Printery.

Biggs, J. (1987). *Student approaches to learning and studying.* Melbourne: Australian Council for Educational Research.

Biggs, J. B., and Telfer, R. (1987). *The process of learning.* Sydney: Prentice Hall.

Bowden, J. (1988). Achieving change in teaching practices. In P. Ramsden (Ed.), *Improving Learning*. London: Kogan Page.

Bowden, J. A. (1989, November). Curriculum development for conceptual change learning: A phenomenographic pedagogy. Paper presented to the sixth annual conference of the Hong Kong Educational Research Association, Hong Kong.

Bowden, J. A. (Ed.).(1986). *Student learning: Research into practice.* Melbourne: Melbourne University Press.

Carr, W., and Kemmis, S. (1986). *Becoming critical: Education, knowledge and action research.* Brighton, Sussex: Falmer Press.

Eizenberg, N. (1986). Applying student learning research to practice. In J. Q. Bowden (Ed.), *Student Learning: Research into Practice.* Melbourne: Melbourne University Press.

Gow, L., and Kember, D. (1990). Does higher education promote independent learning? *Higher Education, 19,* 307-322.

Holtz, H. (1989). Action in place of silence: A response to Gimenez. *Teaching Sociology, 17,* 192-193.

Kember, D., and Gow, L. (1989). A model of student approaches to learning encompassing ways to influence and change approaches. *Instructional Science, 18,* 263-288.

Perry, W. G. (1988). Different worlds in the same classroom. In P. Ramsden (Ed.), *Improving Learning: New Perspectives.* London: Kogan Page.

Ramsden, P. (1987). Improving teaching and learning in higher education: The case for a relational perspective. *Studies in Higher Education, 12*(3), 275-286.

Ramsden, P. (Ed.).(1988). *Improving learning: New perspectives. London: Kogan Page.*

Richey, R. (1986). *The theoretical and conceptual bases of instructional design.* London: Kogan Page.

Roth, K., and Anderson, D. (1988). Promoting conceptual change learning from science textbooks. In P. Ramsden (Ed.), *Improving Learning: New Perspectives.* London: Kogan Page.

Schuell, T. J. (1986). Cognitive conceptions of learning. *Review of Educational Research, 56*(4), 411-436.

West, L. H. T., and Pines, A. L. (Eds.).(1985). *Cognitive structure and conceptual change.* New York: Academic Press.

Variety Of Instructional Resources

A college instructor's role has changed tremendously in recent years. As the role moves from lecturer to facilitator, director of active learning activities, and planner, the instructional resources must also change. In order to accommodate the new diverse role of "teacher," the diverse role of student and the diverse characteristics of college students, a teacher must utilize the necessary tools to be effective. The effective teacher uses a variety of materials.

In deciding which resources to use, teachers need to consider the following: teacher objectives, student population, physical facilities, and assessment.

Below is a list of resources and suggestions for use:

1. *Blackboard*
   a. *Teacher Objectives:* If your objective is to determine *comprehension*, then the blackboard is an effective tool for students to work math and physical science problems. Too, it is effective for displaying a lesson outline or the class objectives.
   b. *Student Population:* The board is effective for *visual learners.* It actually impedes auditory learners because the sound of the chalk on board interferes with learning. It is not an effective resource for students with learning disabilities because the distance from the desk to the blackboard blocks concentration.
   c. *Disadvantages:* Most students sitting in the back of the classroom have problems reading the board and tend to "tune out"; the board becomes cluttered very quickly and using it becomes counter productive; writing on the board is time-consuming; writing on the board requires your back being turned

to students; chalk dust exacerbates allergies; teachers generally write too small; and, teachers tend to stand in the way of the material on the board.

2. *Overhead Projectors*

   a. *Teacher Objectives:* If your objective is to determine comprehension or supplement knowledge, an overhead projector is quite effective.

   A transparency used as a knowledge supplement can be made months ahead of its scheduled use. This allows the instructor the luxury of more effective planning and a more flexible curriculum. Too, transparencies are quite durable and will last for several semesters. A transparency is also an excellent assessment tool. Having students fill in a concept map or complete a skeletal outline at the end of a lesson can alert the instructor to the degree of or lack of comprehension.

   b. *Student Population:* The overhead projector is effective for visual learners. When a transparency is coupled with an oral commentary, it is also effective for auditory learners. When students must actually complete a concept map or outline from a transparency, the kinesthetic learner is also activated. The overhead, then, has the potential to meet the needs of all learners.

   c. *Disadvantages:* The writing on many canned transparencies is way too small for classroom use. As a result, students sitting in the back are often frustrated because they can't read the information. Two other disadvantages include the necessity for an outlet in close proximity and for an extra bulb should the one on the overhead blow. Some students with Attention Deficit Disorder find the hum of the overhead and its glare distracting. Last, transparencies and markers are rather expensive and supplies are usually limited.

3. *Handouts*

   a. *Teacher Objectives:* If your objective is to supplement *knowledge,* provide a source for comparison/contrast for *analysis,* provide an extra component for *synthesis,* then handouts are beneficial.

    b. *Student Population:* Handouts are effective for *visual learners.* Unless the teacher actually reviews the handout, it will not be an effective resource for the auditory and kinesthetic learners.

    c. *Disadvantages:* If the importance of the handout is not stressed or the student has no idea why the handout was given, handouts tend to wind up merely being kept, not read or used.

4. **Computers**

    a. *Teacher Objectives:* Computers can lend themselves to higher order thinking skills such as application, analysis, synthesis, and evaluation. Examples of computer learning projects include using word processing for research papers; using videodiscs to illustrate art and literature relationships; using software for drill and practice tutorials; using software for graphics, desktop publishing, and spreadsheets; testing; instructional simulations; educational games; problem solving; and low-incidence courses (Johansen, 1993).

    b. *Student Population:* The independent, kinesthetic learner benefits the most from this resource; however, computers accommodate all learning styles. Learning disabled students, especially those with dysgraphia or dyslexia, show a high rate of success with this resource (Bogart, Eidelman, Kujawa, 1988).

    c. *Disadvantages:* There are not enough computers, so scheduling the computer lab for classroom instruction is difficult, if not impossible. It takes time to preview software, and much software or computer capability is obsolete before fully used.

5. *Instructional Television, Video Cassettes, Camcorders*

    a. *Teacher Objectives:* To trigger feelings and reactions; to supplement information; to evaluate performance; to analyze experiments; to bring the world into the classroom; and, to analyze, diagnose, and correct problems are possible objectives for these tools.

    b. *Student Population:* These tools enhance all learning styles because they supply a concrete basis for conceptual thinking and have a high degree of interest for all students.

       c. *Disadvantages:* These resources are in short supply because they are expensive, and the tendency to overuse is present without careful planning.

6. *Models—Skeletons, Machinery, Globes*

       a. *Teacher Objectives:* To demonstrate, to reconstruct, to analyze, to compare/contrast, to simulate are objectives of these resources.

       b. *Student Population:* These resources help all types of learners but particularly help the kinesthetic learner and the learning disabled. If students are not formal operational thinkers, these resources are invaluable as they provide the bridge from abstract concept to concrete application.

       c. *Disadvantages:* To be truly effective, all students need the opportunity to manipulate the models. Lessons must be carefully planned so that everyone stays involved while turns are taken with the models. Ideally, each group of four students would have a model.

7. *Speakers*

       a. *Teacher Objectives:* If the teacher's objectives include supplementing information, reinforcing information with an "expert" from the field, to compare/contrast, to evaluate different viewpoints, speakers can be invaluable. Suggestions for use would include a K-4 math specialist explaining math reform assessment techniques to prospective elementary teachers, an engineer who could provide real life application of calculus, a business CEO explaining new management techniques to a business management class, etc.

       b. *Student Population:* Any student can benefit from a speaker as long as the teacher's objectives are clearly stated.

       c. *Disadvantages:* Careful planning is required to coordinate the contribution of the resource person with the sequence of work that students are doing in the classroom.

8. *Simulation Games*

       a. *Teacher Objectives*: To create, to apply, to evaluate, to reinforce are all objectives of simulation games. Simulation games such as playing the stock market, creating a newspaper, running a mock business are all excellent ways to facilitate the transition from school to work.

   b. *Student Population:* All students can benefit from simulation games provided the objectives are clearly stated, evaluation is constructed to match the objectives, and everyone participates.

   c. *Disadvantages:* Requires much pre-planning and playing time.

9. *Supplies as Resources*—Inexpensive supplies can often be one of the most beneficial classroom resources. Examples are given below:

   a. *Butcher paper and markers*—a pictorial representation of information is very beneficial to the kinesthetic learner. For example, to read about how a K-3 classroom should look and be arranged takes on a much greater significance when the words are transported to a picture of the room. Preparing a continuous historical time line with pictures of significant events placed along the way as they are studied is an immensely helpful study guide. Drawing a cell and labeling its parts or designing examples of math formulas and calculations placed on butcher paper and posted to the wall reinforces learning.

   b. *Objects for object lessons*—food containers to measure, evaluate for advertising effectiveness, examine list of ingredients for health evaluation, or to make art objects. Any object has the potential for becoming a teaching tool.

   c. *Colored paper, colored transparencies*—these tools help the learning disabled student. Color focuses the words and holds them stable.

   d. *Manila folders and index cards*—using manila folders for portfolio assessment is a timely educational tool. With the current thrust on authentic assessment, portfolios provide both student and teacher with an on-going performance evaluation. Students become adept at evaluating the quality of their own work. Index cards are invaluable for grouping students, writing review questions, writing a summary of the class, and for providing the means for a quick assessment.

References

Bogart, S., Eidelman, L., and Kujawa, C. (1993, January). Helping learning-disabled students in college. *The Education Digest,* 48-51.

Johansen, J., Johnson, J., and Henniger, M. (1993). *American education: An introduction to teaching.* Dubuque: Wm. C. Brown Communications, Inc.

Motivation

Motivation is defined as the forces that account for the arousal, selection, direction, and continuation of behavior (Biehler and Snowman, 1993). Ideally, by the time students are working at the college level, the desire to become one of Maslow's self-actualizers is sufficient motivation. Realistically, however, we know this is not the case. In fact, our students vary significantly in academic abilities and in interests and attitudes toward work and authority. Also, extrinsic attractions are widespread in our culture, and many students are influenced by a reward as an immediate gratification. As a result, few students have the capacity for self-reinforcement (Lowman, 1990).

The problem is then compounded because true motivation, is intrinsic; it must come from within a person, so the most a teacher can do is to create the circumstances that influence students to want to learn.

Many factors influence a student's inclination to learn—the nature of the learning task, characteristics of individual pupils, classroom atmosphere, and the personality and delivery method of the teacher.

A. *Nature of the Learning Task* - If the subject were self-selected, there is a built-in interest and motivation. If, however, the subject is required with little interest or appeal, the teacher must create circumstances to foster interest.

Suggestions for Teaching in Your Classroom:

1. Make class as active, useful, and social as possible.
2. Cooperative learning, projects, presentations, simulations, guest speakers, and field trips are examples of ways to make learning active.

B. *Characteristics of Individual Students* - Some of your students may have never experienced academic success, some may have learning disabilities, some may suffer test anxiety, some will be divergent thinkers, and some may have had embarrassing or humiliating classroom experiences.

Suggestions for Teaching in Your Classroom:

1. Make sure each student is initially successful in your classroom. This can be interpreted any number of ways; however, one success does lead to another because it builds self-confidence along the way. Intrinsically, students will be motivated because they will feel a sense of accomplishment and will desire to repeat those positive feelings. Ways to ensure success might include discussion leader, peer tutor, presenter, reporter, making a project, designing a project, etc.

2. Perhaps as many as one-third (see section on Student Variability) of your students will suffer from some type of learning disability. Have students write you a letter the first day which includes these components:

   a. Describe yourself without using physical features.
   b. What do you expect to get out of this class?
   c. What do you expect from me?
   d. What can I do to make learning easier or more comfortable for you?

   Many times students will take this opportunity to divulge a learning disability or any other concern that will help you address students' individual needs.

3. Teachers who wish to increase their students' motivation should be concerned about their evaluation and assessment methods. Teachers who over-emphasize exams as external ordeals by making them difficult to complete in the allotted amount of time, "tricky" by their own admission, or administering so few that one test has the power "to make or break" a student's grade severely impairs students' motivation. Teachers can use evaluation methods that encourage conceptual learning. For example, portfolio assessments; essay application problems; collaborative tests; half take-home, half in-class tests; student-made tests and study guides; and mastery learning may be used to promote motivation. Too, Eison's research with learning orientation and grading orientation (1981) demonstrated that even though faculty

members advocate intrinsic motivation, they often unwittingly encourage extrinsic because of an emphasis on grades. For example, using grades to control nonacademic behavior (lowering grades for absences or late work) encourages a grading orientation. Using evaluations for the purpose of instructive feedback, assigning ungraded work, and reminding students of everything they have learned encourage intrinsic motivation.

4. Establish a comfortable learning environment in which students know the teacher is on their side and wants them to succeed. Lowman (1990) feels motivation can be increased by avoiding subtle or blatant remarks that promote faculty power over students. For instance, when teachers joke about the difficulty of their exams (Don't worry about making an A; just hope you all don't make F's—hah-hah!") they emphasize their power to give rewards or punishments.

C. *Classroom Atmosphere* - A cooperative-learning classroom seems to promote intrinsic motivation according to one study (Benware and Deci, 1984). This is not surprising since cooperative learning promotes less risk to an individual. Too, if students know they are responsible for the learning of another, they will be more intrinsically motivated to prepare in order to do a good job. An atmosphere that fosters cooperative learning between the teacher and the student is also conducive to motivation. If students have some say or choice in the construction of the class, in the content of the course, and in the evaluation method of the course, they will feel an integral part of the classroom.

Suggestions for Teaching in Your Classroom:

1. Learn names as quickly as possible.

2. Make it a point to know at least one personal bit of information about each student (children, work, hobbies, etc.), so you can discuss something other than course work with the student.

3. Rigid rows imply a rigid teacher-centered classroom. Use semicircles or circles when appropriate to promote inclusiveness in classroom.

4. Build camaraderie among students by having students take responsibility for one student in the class. The two students

exchange personal information on the first day of class (telephone number, address, etc.). For the rest of the semester, those students call when one is absent, take notes for each other, and become a support system.

5. Continually point out that what is being learned can be used outside of class.

6. Make sure students know exactly what is expected of them so that they can succeed.

7. Be alert for physical annoyances and try to eliminate (too hot, too cold, noise in hall, etc.).

D. *Teacher Personality and Delivery:*

1. McKeachie (1986) indicates that the enthusiasm of the lecturer is an important factor in affecting student learning and motivation. An enthusiastic teacher exudes optimism, a positive attitude, and self-confidence. These traits are contagious!

2. A teacher who displays active listening skills invites student participation and promotes motivation.

3. A teacher who keeps her students engaged promotes motivation.

Suggestions for Teaching in Your Classroom:

1. If you are not enthusiastic about the day, the lesson, or the students, never let the students know. Do not whine, complain, or reprimand in the classroom. These produce a ripple effect which affects all members. Participation will halt abruptly.

2. Be an active listener by giving full attention to the speaker, making eye contact, and asking questions. Make an appointment with the student if time does not allow for adequate response.

3. Keeping students engaged is the hardest, most time-consuming but most rewarding of all the motivational factors. Engagement depends on the type of delivery used and how the information is delivered.

   a. Verbal reinforcement is important to any delivery technique. Simple comments such as "way to go," "well done," or an "exemplary paper" can be powerful motivators (Rubadeau, 1984). Praise increases the probability that the student will work hard to achieve at that level on future tasks; however, research suggests that the outgoing, self-confident student responds better to statements implying that you expected a better performance ("I was really surprised at your grade; didn't you get a chance to review?") (Rubadeau, 1984).

b. Surprise—nothing kills motivation like routine. Vary your delivery method. If your usual method is lecture, try having students ask for the information they want from the teacher in the role of "The Grand Pooh-Bah." Students must, of course, know the objectives for the class.

c. Games and simulations provide an excellent means of motivation. Consider having students make a game themselves.

d. Let the student become the teacher and the teacher become the student for a portion of the period. Assign student a certain portion of material to cover. Encourage the student to be as creative as possible. Everest (1990) found that students came to class much better prepared.

Rubadeau (1984) states that it is not enough to provide ways to motivate students; we must reduce existing negative factors which impede motivation. Some of the common *negative* factors include:

- being graded on a curve, in which the student's efforts to achieve the objectives do not make a difference, as only a certain percentage of the students will get the A's and B's.

- where the student's request for assistance from the instructor is not given any attention.

- when the instructor talks down to the students assuming that they are stupid and can't understand the more difficult concepts.

- having an instructor who is bored or burned-out and is not interested in the course material.

- walking in to take an exam that is not based on the objectives for the course or the material that was covered in class.
- attempting to learn material that is way over the head of the student.
- the instructor not taking into account the entry level of the students.
- taking a test that is based on trivia rather than real course content.
- where the instructor has set his/her pace for the really good students and does not seem to care if the rest of the class learns the material.
- not getting exam results or papers back for weeks and weeks after they were turned in.

In trying to motivate his students, Ronald Luce (1990) made the startling discovery that his students were not necessarily unmotivated or unwilling learners; "They are simply uninvolved in the depersonalization of the traditional classroom. They *are* willing to learn; they simply may not be able to endure the way they are taught" (p. 2).

What, then, is the message for college faculty? Faculty should examine their teaching and grading practices and strengthen those that encourage intrinsic motivation.

References

Benware, C., and Deci, E. L. (1984). Quality of learning with an active versus passive motivational set. *American Educational Research Journal, 21*, 755-765.

Biehler, R., and Snowman, J. (1993). *Psychology applied to teaching*. Houghton Mifflin: Boston.

Eison, J. (1981). A new instrument for assessing students' orientations toward grades and learning. *Psychological Reports ,58*, 919-924.

Everest, M. (1990). Creating enthusiasm in the classroom. *Innovation Abstracts, 12*(20).

Lowman, J. (1990). Promoting motivation and learning. *College Teaching*, 38, 136-139.

Luce, R. (1990). Motivating the unmotivated. *Innovation Abstracts, 12*(8).

McKeachie, W. (1986). Teaching and learning in the college classroom. A review of the research literature. National Center for Research to Improve Postsecondary Teaching and Learning, Ann Arbor, MI.

Rubadeau, D. O., and others. (1984). A guide to motivational procedures for instruction. College of New Caledonia, Prince George (British Columbia). Centre for Improved Teaching.

Suggested Reading

Benjamin, M., McKeachie, W. J., Lin, Y. G., and Holinge, D. P. (1981). Text anxiety: Deficits in information processing. *Journal of Educational Psychology.* 73, 816-824.

Beukhof, G., and Simons, R. J. (Eds.). (1986). *German and Dutch research on learning and instruction. General topics and self-regulation in knowledge acquisition. Den Haag: Stichting voor Onderzoek van het Onderwigs.*

Bransford, J., Sherwood, R., Vye, N.,and& Rieser, J. (1986). Teaching thinking and problem solving: Research foundations. *American Psychologist, 41*(10), 1078-1089.

Deci, E. L. (1971). Effects of externally mediated rewards on intrinsic motivation. *Journal of Personality and Social Psychology, 18*: 105-115.

Deci, E. L. (1975). *Intrinsic motivation.* New York: Plenum.

Deci, E. L., and Ryan, R. M. (1985). *Intrinsic motivation and self-determination in human behavior.* New York: Plenum.

Derry, S. J., Hawkes, L. W., and Tsal, C. J. (1987). A theory for remediating problem solving skills of older children and adults. *Educational Psychologist.* 22(1), 1089.

Emery, G. (1982). *Own your own life.* New York: New American Library.

Freidrich, H. F., and Mandl, H. (1986). Self-regulation in knowledge acquisition: A selection of German research. In G. Beukhof & R. J. Simons (Eds.), German and Dutch research on learning and instruction: General topics and self-regulation in knowledge acquisition (43-99). Den Haag: Stichting voor Onderzoek van het Onderwijs.

Isen, A. M., Daubman, K. A., and Kowicki, G. P. (1987). Positive affect facilitates creative problem solving. *Journal of Personality and Social Psychology.* 52(6), 1122-1131.

Langer, E. J., and Piper, A. I. (1987). The prevention of mindlessness. *Journal of Personality and Social Psychology.* (53), 280-287.

Leal, L. (1987). Investigation of the relation between metamemory and university students' examination performance. *Journal of Educational Psychology.* 79(1), 35-40.

Lowman, J. (1984). *Mastering the techniques of teaching.* San Francisco: Jossey-Bass.

McCombs, B. L. (1986). The role of the self-system in self-regulated learning. Paper presented at AERA symposium. San Francisco.

McCombs, B. L. (1987, April). The role of affective variables in autonomous learning. Paper presented at AERA meeting. Washington, DC.

McCombs, B. L. (1987, August). Preliminary validation of a battery of primary motivational process variables. Paper presented at American Psychological Association meeting. New York.

McKeachie, W. J., Pintrich, P. R., Lin, Y. G., and Smith, D. A. F. (1986). Teaching and learning in the college classroom: A review of the research literature (Tech. Rep. No.

86-0B-001.01). Ann Arbor, MI: University of Michigan. National Center for Research to Improve Postsecondary Teaching and Learning.

Milton, O., Pollio, H. R., and Eison, J. A. (1986). *Making sense of college grades.* San Francisco: Jossey-Bass.

Naveh-Benjamin, M. (1985). Test anxiety: Effects of improving study habits and systematic desensitization. Paper presented at American Psychological Association convention. Los Angeles.

Naveh-Benjamin, M., McKeachie, W. J., and Linn, Y. G. (1987). Two types of text-anxious students: Support for an information processing model. *Journal of Education Psychology, 79*(2), 131-136.

Nisbett, R. E., Fong, G. T., Lehman, D., and Cheng, P. W. (1987). Teaching reasoning. *Science,* 238, 625-631.

Pressley, M., Cariglta-Bull, T., and Snyder, B. (1984). Are there programs that can really teach thinking and learning skills? *Contemporary Educational Review,* 3, 435-444.

Sagerman, N., and Mayer, R. E. (1987). Forward transfer of different reading strategies evoked by adjunct questions in science text. *Journal of Educational Psychology, 79*(2), 189-191.

Segal, J. W., Chipman, S. F., and Glaser, R. (Eds.).(1985). Thinking and learning skills, Vol. I: Relating instruction to research. Hillsdale, NJ: L. Erlbaum Assocs.

Simmons, R. J., and Vermunt, J. D. H. M. (1986). Self-regulation in knowledge acquisition: A selection of Dutch research. In G. Beukhof & R. J. Simons (Eds.). German and Dutch research on learning and instruction: General topics and self-regulation in knowledge acquisition (101-135). Den Haag: Stichting voor Onderzoek van het Onderwijs.

Steers, R. M., and Porter, L. W. (1987). *Motivation and work behavior.* (4th ed.). New York: McGraw-Hill.

Tec, L. (1980). *Targets: How to set goals for yourself and teach them.* New York: Signet Books.

Tobias, S. (1987). Mandatory text review and interaction with student characteristics. *Journal of Educational Psychology.* 79(2), 154-161.

Waern, Y., and Rabenius, L. (1987). Metacognitive aspects of learning difficult texts. In E. DeCorte, H. Lodewijks, R. Parmentier, and P. Span (Eds.). Learning and instruction: European research in an international context: Vol. I. Oxford: Pergamon/Leuven University.

Communication Skills

The instructor's ability to deliver clear and skillful verbal and non-verbal messages which enhance student learning is rarely given prominence in current discussions of the dimensions of teaching excellence. However, research describing students' perceptions of teaching behaviors, as reported on the Teaching Analysis by Students (TABS) questionnaire, clearly indicates that students perceive the teacher's organization and presentation skills as a major dimension of teaching behavior (Kerwin, 1989). Furthermore, though students closely link organization and presentation skills, they evaluate them separately from other teaching behaviors such as student involvement and interpersonal relation skills. Although a number of behaviors are included in the dimension of organization and presentation, clearly both verbal and nonverbal aspects of communication are key factors in effective classroom presentation. This most basic attribute of teaching must not be overlooked in our haste to ascribe to current teaching innovations.

In reviewing current literature, McKeachie, et.al. (1987) conclude that enthusiasm, expressiveness, energy, and instructor commitment make a difference in achieving most educational goals. It is interesting to note that a definite link to communication skill is seen in the top five responses of students when asked to describe the characteristics of "outstanding" instructors: knowledge of subject, well organized, concerned about and responsive to student needs, enthusiasm for subject, and friendly and personable (Magnesen and Parker, 1986). A correlation has been shown between student achievement, motivation, and attendance; and instructor enthusiasm and expressiveness as demonstrated by behaviors such as movement, gestures, eye contact, voice inflection, minimal reliance on lecture notes and use of relevant humor (Schonwetter, 1993). Skilled classroom communication can be described as including: (1) strategies for communicating to establish rapport and connection with students; (2) nonverbal communication strategies; and, (3) instructional planning for effective classroom communication.

Communicating for Rapport and Connection

A worthwhile exercise for instructors to engage in periodically is a careful reflection on the teachers of our past, who engaged our love of their subject matter and inspired our best efforts, as well as those who turned us off or failed to stimulate our personal involvement with the subject. Most often we remember the former as those for whom we felt a personal connection, a sense that the student, above all else, was the really important ingredient in that classroom.

Instructors who establish rapport and connection are attuned to the joy of watching students learn and are personally motivated by an appreciation of the importance of their teaching to the lives of their students. They view teaching as an activity done with students, sharing with the learners the responsibility of creating a worthwhile learning experience (Cartwright, 1989). While this is largely a state of mind or an attitude we adopt, there are concrete classroom strategies that convey this message to the students.

Strategies for the Classroom:

- Approach the class with a sense of mutual respect. Develop a sense of expecting the best and giving your best in each class session. Listeners will support a speaker they see as honest, sincere, and concerned about their welfare.
- Indicate your respect early in the class session by starting promptly and letting students know that you recognize and appreciate the knowledge and experience that they bring to the class.
- Encourage an atmosphere that is open and relaxed. Tell the class that you expect the session to be give-and-take. Invite students to ask questions. Rather than, "Are there any questions?", ask students to think of and share one unanswered question.
- Maintain a focus on the students rather than content. Never read to students; it automatically becomes one-way communication. Teach from an outline, not detailed notes; you'll be more sponta-

neous. Using as few notes as possible also signals to the students that you are comfortable with your subject and this gives you credibility.

- Develop a personal relationship with students. While this, of course, has its appropriate boundaries, strategies such as providing time at the beginning of a class term for both teacher and students to share a bit of their background and consistently arriving to class early to converse with individual students motivate students to enter into a commitment to collaborate with the instructor.

- Be available to students outside of class time and take the initiative to invite students to meet with you personally for one-on-one help or just to share perceptions of the course and their role in the class.

- Be vulnerable in sharing a relevant personal story or experience that portrays you as real and genuine and creates a classroom atmosphere of honesty, openness and integrity.

- Learn the students' names early in the term and use them often. This is so critical to establishing connection that it is worth the investment of time and energy, even in large classes. Memory games and gimmicks or even photographing students for some instructor "homework" will not only be tolerated but actually appreciated by students as they see your sincerity in approaching them as individuals.

- Be positive in your response to feedback and questions, even when these are less than desired. Keep in mind that your treatment of any one member of the class sends messages of respect and acceptance for all members.

- As you get to know your students, accompany key points with analogies or specific, real-life examples taken from their areas of interest and experience.

Nonverbal Communication in the Classroom

Classroom instruction is something you do, a skill to develop. The task of effectively engaging a classroom of individuals at the same time and location for numerous class meetings over the duration of the term requires the communicator to develop a "presentation presence."

This public presence may be different from that you project in one-on-one conversation but allows you to show forcefully that enthusiasm you feel for the subject. Much of the message you portray in this presence is delivered by the nonverbal aspects of speech. Nonverbal messages play a great part in the way an audience reacts to you. Incidentals such as dress, gestures, pacing, shifting, eye contact, loudness, and tone of voice may be deciding factors in student perceptions and the degree in which they engage themselves with you in the learning process (Bishop, 1985). Research conducted in speaker credibility suggests that today's audiences are more influenced by the speaker's energy level than by degree of knowledge of the subject matter (Peterson, 1989). As inappropriate as that may seem, it simply means that low-key classroom style works against a classroom instructor. Fortunately, a few simple strategies can be developed to match the instructor enthusiasm for the subject with the classroom presence.

Strategies for the Classroom:

- Practice noticing and interpreting student nonverbal messages. If you see a negative reaction or a confused look, use the opportunity to stop and expand on the point or to elicit questions, without putting any one individual on the spot.
- Develop nonverbal behaviors that convey a sense of enthusiasm in the classroom. That is, keep smiling, be energetic but not distracting in movement and hand gestures, elevate your voice and change its pitch and tone throughout the delivery.
- Use pauses skillfully. Planned pauses are effective signals just before you state a key point, just after you state a key point, between items on a list, and after introducing new terminology. Use a lengthy pause just before moving on to another topic. You may even move to a new location of the room or quickly clear the board. This gives an opportunity for student thought to catch up with your delivery and assures that the students can make those transitions with you. Be careful to provide adequate wait time both after a question and following the student response to engage all the students in that exchange.

- Vary the pace of a lecture. Speak more slowly and deliberately on the major points and pick up the pace on the more minor supportive information.

- Use the volume of your voice to signal important information; either turning up the volume or lowering it to a whisper can be powerful attention grabbers.

- Use spatial expression to stimulate learners visually as well as aurally. Move in toward students for key points or to signal that you want to hear from them. Move to the side when elaborating or providing examples. However, moving too close to a student or group of students engaged in discussion can have a negative effect: they quit talking. Moving close to students who are providing distraction in class will usually bring a halt to such behavior without interrupting the class activity.

- Place the overhead projector or other visual aids a few feet away from you. This forces you to walk to them and back to your audience, providing you with some frequent opportunities for movement.

- Convey a sense of organization by maintaining a clean board surface. Erase the entire board after each main section of the presentation. Besides signifying the end of a topic, this allows you to create new space and removes distractions and possible future interruptions.

- Carefully examine your class presence for any distracting mannerisms. If possible, have a class session videotaped and look for verbal and nonverbal habits which may create distractions for the learners. This is also an excellent means of evaluating your overall nonverbal presence in the classroom.

- Write "stage directions" into your class outlines. Short notations such as "pause here," "walk to side of room," or "raise voice for emphasis" may seem artificial at first but are excellent reminders for you as you start to build more nonverbal behaviors into your teaching style.

Instructional Planning for Effective Classroom Communication

Instructional planning includes more than setting objectives, writing a syllabus and choosing media. It is possible to structure a class from beginning to end in a way that conveys its importance to the students. Following are six strategies to gain immediately students' interest and attention (Chapman, 1991):

1. Have a problem set up and waiting for participants. Announce that you're having a contest and the first person to solve the problem wins a prize (be creative, even silly).

2. Build a bridge between information presented before and what is to come or link the topic to a current event.

3. Share with the class a tangible accomplishment they will achieve before the class session is over.

4. Conduct a short class survey to find out what knowledge or experience they already have or opinions they hold concerning the day's topic.

5. Convey the message that you and the room are ready for this class. That is, be in the classroom before students arrive and meet them with a smile and greeting. Have handouts, overheads, chalk, etc., ready and at hand. Have tables and chairs arranged and change this arrangement from time to time if possible.

6. Use a structured icebreaker activity to begin class. Icebreakers can pave the way for the main subject area and help students begin to feel comfortable with new information. They can set the tone for the group dynamics you want to achieve in that class and put students at ease with talking to each other and working together. Students who regularly engage in icebreaker activities tend to be well connected to each other and the instructor (Berry, 1994).

Once you have their attention and interest, plan to continue to involve the learners in the communication process. While there is a variety of student participation techniques which can be used to encourage active learning, a critical element in successful student involvement is the nurturing of an atmosphere which supports interpersonal communication (Mamchur, 1989). This can be achieved by focusing on the learners rather than the content and by empowering the learners. The question to ask before the class session, then, is "What do I want the learner to accomplish" rather than, "What do I want to cover." We need to focus on what we, as instructors, can do to help students recognize their own valuable knowledge and experience and leave class recognizing what they have accomplished and what they can do with this new knowledge. After all, it is this conviction and enthusiasm that we each feel for our field of study that motivated us to develop expertise. Classroom assessment techniques (Angelo and Cross, 1993) can be excellent vehicles for encouraging student self discovery. For example, asking students to create a focused list of the key issues or points in a lesson's content tells not only you, but them, what they have learned and can take away from this session. As a bonus, more often than not, they will reinforce the very items you wish to emphasize. Even the simple 10-2, 10-2 format (10 minutes of presentation, 2 minutes of buzz groups) is effective. These types of activities create an atmosphere that says, "Your ideas count."

Finally, planning opportunities for humor in the classroom is an effective communication strategy. Humor can enliven the classroom experience, ease tension, raise the energy level of the class, and enhance the student's perception of instructor accessibility. Humor makes material easier for students to remember (Cartwright, 1989, and Goodman, 1983). Appropriate classroom humor may include jokes, if they illustrate a point you are wanting to make, but may also include cartoons, funny photographs, skits, stories, readings, and quotations. Exaggeration can illustrate a point in a humorous way. Sometimes it is helpful to see in an exaggerated way how *not* to do something. For many instructors, humor just doesn't flow naturally. However, even the most subdued personalities can plan a cartoon on an overhead transparency for a strategic transitional point in the lesson, or create a "humor" bulletin board in the classroom. Students may be invited to bring with them a humorous quotation, joke, or perspective on the day's topic. Humor, of course, must be used with sensitivity. Appropriate humor may poke fun at universal human foibles but does not reinforce stereotypes or single out a particular group.

References

Angelo, Thomas A. and Cross, K. P.(1993). *Classroom Assessment Techniques: A Handbook for College Teaching*, (2nd ed.). San Francisco: Jossey-Bass.

Berry, Bart A. (1994). Breaking the ice. *Training and Development 48*(2), 19-23.

Bishop, K. A. (1985, June). The Silent Signals. *Training and Development Journal*, . 36.

Cartwright, L. (1989). Enhancing your enthusiasm. *Innovation Abstracts, 6*(19).

Chapman, T., et.al. (1991). Polish your presentations. *Training and Development 45*(7), 23-27.

Goodman, J. (1983). Using humor in workshops. *The Annual for Facilitators, Trainers, and Consultants. San Diego, CA: University Associates, Inc.*

Kerwin, M. A. (1989). Analyzing student-perceived teaching behavior using the Teaching Analysis by Students questionnaire (TABS). *Journal of Staff, Program and Organizational Development, 7*(3), 115-119.

Kiechel, W. (1987, August). Learn how to listen. *Fortune*, 107-108.

Louw, A. (1986, August). Stage fright: how to break your own barriers and become a more effective presenter. *Training*, 55-57.

McKeachie, W. J., et.al. (1987). *Teaching and learning in the college classroom: a review of the research literature.* National Center for Research to Improve Postsecondary Teaching and Learning, University of Michigan, Ann Arbor, MI.

Magnan, B.(Ed). (1989). *147 Practical Tips for Teaching Professors.* Magna Publications, Inc., Madison, WI.

Magnesen, V. and Parker, L. (1986). Is it wizardry or magic? What makes an outstanding teacher? *Innovation Abstracts, 7*(28).

Mamchur, C. (1989). Connecting with your audience. *College Teaching, 37*(2), 46-48.

Peterson, J. (1989). Improving classroom communication. *Innovation Abstracts, 11*(27).

Schonwetter, D. J. (1993). Attributes of effective lecturing in the college classroom. *The Canadian Journal of Higher Education, 13*(2), 1-18.

Suggested Reading

Berry, S. E. and Garmston, R. J. (1987, January). Become a state-of-the-art presenter. *Training and Development Journal*, 19-22.

Dallmann-Jones, A.S., et.al. (1994). *The Expert Educator: A Reference Manual of Teaching Strategies for Quality Education.* Three Blue Herons Publishing, Inc., Fond du Lac, WI.

McKeachie, W. J. (1986). *Teaching Tips: A guidebook for the beginning college teacher.* (8th ed.). Boston: D. C. Heath.

Murray, H. G. (1985). Classroom teaching behaviors related to college teaching effectiveness. In J. G. Donald and A. M. Sullivan (Eds.), Using research to improve teaching. *New Directions for Teaching and Learning*, No. 23. San Francisco: Jossey-Bass.

Witrock, M. (Ed.).(1986). *Handbook of Research on Teaching* (3rd ed.). New York: Macmillian Publishing Company.

Variety of Methods

College teaching is drastically changing directions. Once exclusively didactic, delivering the teacher's expertise via the lecture, teaching is now more facilitative, using techniques that are dependent not upon the teacher's expertise, but rather on an understanding of how people learn. Even though the lecture remains the foundation teaching method, the authors of several national reports (Assoc. of American Colleges, 1985; Study Group on the Conditions of Excellence in American Higher Education, 1984) have cited the overuse of lecture as a factor which inhibits students' learning and have suggested that faculty develop other teaching methods. In his Paideia Proposal, Adler (1982) maintained that "All genuine learning is active, not passive. It involves the use of the mind, not just the memory. It is a process of discovery in which the student is the main agent, not the teacher" (p. 23). In choosing a teaching method for a class period, the teacher must first ask the questions, "What is it exactly that I want my students to know and to be able to do?" Once answered, the teacher should choose a method which will accomplish those objectives.

1. *Lecture*—If the lecture method is the best vehicle for accomplishing the moment's objective, prepare a detailed lesson plan (Schlenker and Perry, 1986) which contains an introduction, presentation, and summary.

    a. The introduction should include the title of the lecture, the objectives stating what students should be able to do at the end of the lesson, the evaluation to be used for mastery of the objectives, and an overview of the lesson and value of the lesson.

    b. The presentation should include an outline of the sequence of events, as well as questions you plan to ask and activities you plan to do.

    c. The summary indicates how you plan to review the main points as well as any evaluation methods or reinforcement application.

To ensure maximum effectiveness, share the objectives and presentation outline with the students. You may use the board, an overhead, or a flip chart. This allows students to know what you think is important, helps them to distinguish major and minor points for test questions, and facilitates their notetaking.

2. *Simulations*—Situations in which students practice for the real world but are not a part of the real world are simulations. These include role play, games, and case studies.

    a. Role play allows students to practice new behaviors in a safe setting and to develop insight into their own and others' behaviors. Usually role play involves two to six people, takes from five to twenty minutes and may be either structured or spontaneous. Examples of use may include participants demonstrating interviewing techniques, client conflict, taking on the persona of someone else to explain different conceptual viewpoints such as those of Piaget, Van Gogh, Maria Montessori, Martin Luther King, etc. Tips for making this useful method work include:

        (1) Ascertain the purpose of the simulation. Ask yourself, "What is it I want my students to know and be able to do?"

        (2) Design a script to reflect your objectives.

        (3) Outline the scenario.

        (4) Give feedback.

        (5) Solicit feedback from class.

    b. *Games*—Teachers and students can make their own or purchase games such as Prisoner's Dilemma, a management training game; Simsoc, a social relationship game; Blue/Green, a business game which illustrate the concept of competition and cooperation among departments. Helaine Alessio (1991) created ECG Attack to assist students in learning cardiovascular physiology and electrocardiography interpretation. She used the game to reinforce information presented in lectures and reading assignments. She suggests similar approaches could be used in other disciplines. For example, a game for a history course might involve spaces on the game board representing a series of historical events in chronological order. By advancing along the game board, players could become familiar with important events in time. Another example is a game for a geography course. The game board could be set inside a map with players moving throughout a region; consequently, they could become familiar with the locations of cities, battle sites, or geographical terrain.

c. *Case Studies*—A case is a story; it presents the concrete narrative detail of actual, or at least realistic, events. Boehrer and Linsky (1990) feel that addressing a realistic problem as if it were one's own invokes the natural process of acquiring knowledge and skill, not for their own sake but for their contribution to reaching an objective. The knowledge that results tends to remain active and usable, distinct from inert knowledge acquired through more traditional methods. Case study discussion gives students the opportunity to practice or work on their own professional issues in a protected environment under a teacher's supervision. Cases foster critical thinking, transfer responsibility for learning from teacher to student, blend affective and cognitive learning, enliven the classroom, and develop collaborative skills.

3. *Cooperative Learning and Teaching*—According to a wealth of evidence, students taught in small discussion groups without a teacher (peer teaching), is extremely effective for a wide range of goals, content, and students of different levels and personalities (McKeachie, 1986). Peer learning/teaching can take different forms. Ideally, a small group is comprised of four to five students, preferably a random selection. Since many college students have limited experience working in a group, group members will have to be taught group behavior as well as be assigned a specific role in the group. For instance, a small group conducting an experiment might contain the reader, the recorder, the facilitator, and the checker. Depending on the teacher and the task, roles would vary. Most important, however, would be clear, concise job descriptions for each role to avoid confusion. Small groups seem to work

because students are affectively involved with the material—not just cognitively. Too, small groups promote worthwhile discussion, individuality, rapport, and cooperation (Herr, 1989).

Evaluation is an area of crucial concern for both faculty and students. There must be individual accountability to eliminate the coasters and/or the dominators. There must also be a vested interest in the group—a reason to want to help others. Although a significant portion of the grade must reflect individual learning, final grades could be based on a combination of individual performance, group performance, and peer evaluation. Cooperative learning can be used effectively at all grade levels (K through graduate school) and in any discipline. Millis (1990) outlines some specific strategies particularly useful for post-secondary classrooms including the following:

a. *Think-Pair-Share*—The instructor poses a question and gives students a minute to think of a response. Students then turn to their partners and share responses. Last, responses are shared with a larger group or entire class during the follow-up discussion.

b. *Three-Step Interview*—Common as an ice-breaker or a team-building exercise, this structure can also be used to share ideas such as hypotheses or reactions to a film or article. Students interview one another in pairs, alternating roles. They then share in a four-member learning team, composed of two pairs, the information or insights gleaned from the paired interview.

c. *Numbered Heads Together*—Members of learning teams, usually composed of four individuals, count off: 1, 2, 3, and 4. The teacher poses a question, usually factual in nature, but requiring some higher order thinking skills. Students discuss the question, making certain that every group member knows the answer. The instructor calls a specific number, and the designated team members (1, 2, 3, or 4) respond as group spokesperson. Again students benefit from the verbalization, and the peer coaching helps both the high and the low achievers. Class time is usually better spent because less time is wasted on inappropriate responses and because all students become actively involved with the material. Since no one knows which number the teacher will call, all team members have a vested interest in being able to articulate the appropriate response.

d. *Roundtable*—In this brainstorming technique, students in a learning team write in turn on a single pad of paper, stating their ideas aloud as they write. As the tablet circulates, more and more information is added until various aspects of a topic are explored.

e. *Talking Chips*—To encourage full and equal participation, each team member shares information and contributes to a discussion after placing a talking chip (e.g., a pen, checker index card) in the center of the group. After all students have contributed in random order, they retrieve their chips to begin another round.

f. *Co-op Cards*—Useful for memorization and review, students coach each other using flashcards. Each student prepares a set of flashcards with a question on the front and the answer on the back. When a student answers a question correctly, the partner hands over the card; they continue going through the set until all questions have been answered correctly. The pair then reverse roles, using the second set of questions and answers prepared by the other partner until both students have mastered both sets of questions.

g. *Jigsaw*—The faculty member divides an assignment or topic into four parts with one person from each "home" learning team volunteering to become an "expert" on one of the parts. Four expert teams with members from each home team then work together to master their fourth of the material and to discover the best way to help others learn it. All experts then reassemble in their home learning teams where they teach the other group members.

h. *Structured Controversy*—Team members assume different positions on controversial issues, discussing, researching, and sharing their findings with the group. This technique allows students to explore topics in depth and promotes higher order thinking skills.

    i. *Group Investigation*—Based on six successive stages, cooperative groups investigate topics of mutual interest, planning what they will study, how they will divide the research responsibilities, and how they will synthesize and summarize their findings for the class.

    j. *Dyads*—Students can learn cooperatively in dyads in which they alternate asking and answering questions on commonly read materials. Students read an assignment and write questions dealing with the major points raised in the reading. At the beginning of each class meeting, students are randomly assigned to pairs. A asks the first question. After B answers correctly or is corrected, B asks A a question, etc.

Cooperative learning can be a valuable method for college faculty and is useful when the task is complex, problem solving is required, divergent thinking is desired, critical thinking is needed, long-term retention is needed, and a sense of community is desired. There are few times when cooperative learning is not beneficial.

4. *Presentations*—Thinkers' Cards and Mini Presentations—Judy Downs (1989) says that thinkers' cards with mini presentations is one way to ensure all students are exposed to important ideas in the text without forcing reading through testing. She assigns each student a section of the text which contains an essential concept. Each student is then given a colored 3x5 index card. The student then (1) carefully reads the assigned section and prepares to speak for the author; (2) summarizes the author's major points in three to four complete sentences on one side of the card; (3) discusses in one sentence on the reverse side any issues the author doesn't address; and, (4) develops one thought-provoking question for class discussion, also placing it on the reverse side. At the next class period, students are arranged in a circle. They give a one-to-two-minute oral presentation at their desks summarizing the material. Students then tell issues the author has not addressed and deliver their question for class discussion.

5. *Clustering*—Writing is an effective way to teach course content; Joanna Ambron (1988) found that clustering is an especially effective writing technique which increased her students' mastery

of vocabulary and scientific concepts in her biology classes. First, the students select a dominant word which is written and circled in the middle of the chalkboard. Next, students say any word or phrase evoked by the "nucleus" word. The teacher writes these on the board, circling and connecting to the center circle by an arrow any word obviously related directly to the nucleus. Once the cluster is complete, individual students determine a pattern in the associations. The student then creates a paragraph on one of the connections made during the exercise. This is especially useful in summarizing lectures. For instance, if the day's lecture is on genetics, "genetics" becomes the nucleus, students collabora- tively cluster, and then using the cluster on the board, students are given 10 minutes to summarize the lecture. Students are graded pass/fail on their writing. All pass except those who do not hand in a summary. As a result, writing becomes a tool for learning and not a test. Scientific literacy has resulted because her students can manipulate the vocabulary and concepts; most importantly, they become actively involved with the learning process.

6. *Projects*—Individual or group projects can help students reach the objectives of the course more completely than any other method if they are relevant. With proper reporting and discussion, projects can provide insights to serve the whole class.

7. *Discussion*—Class discussions usually involve the teacher asking questions and the students (usually the same two or three) answer- ing. Discussion is an effective way to assess degree of under- standing or to correct any misconceptions; however, discussion must be structured to engage all students' attention, if not partici- pation. Usually the two or three students who answer sit in the front. This means if your room is arranged in rows, the discussion dies quickly because the dialogue then becomes a conversation between the student and the teacher. No one sitting in the back can hear; they are totally disenfranchised. To promote discussion, arrange the room in a circle or a horseshoe so no one is excluded. Next, have prepared discussion questions which will either pro- mote consensus, play devil's advocate, promote divergent thought, or promote problem-solving.

Some useful strategies for promoting discussion include the following:

a. According to Fisch (1986), trigger films are an effective way to focus the attention of the group and to maximize the involvement of the members in a discussion.
b. Use a current event which relates to the lesson.
c. Use a startling fact or statistic.
d. Use a hypothetical situation.
e. Use a quotation which has significance to lesson (*Bartlett's Quotations* in Reference Section).
f. Use a picture.
g. Use an object for meaning and expansion.

The effectiveness of teaching methods depends upon one's goals. For the goal of factual knowledge, lectures and reading assignments are likely to be as good or better than other methods. For goals of long-term retention, thinking, and motivation, less structured methods involving more student activity are likely to be superior. Time on task is an important variable, but the questions are "What tasks?" "How is the time spent?" If we want students to become more effective in meaningful learning and thinking, they need to spend more time in active, meaningful learning and thinking—not just sitting passively receiving information.

References

Adler, M. J. (1982). *The padeia proposal: An educational manifesto.* New York: Macmillan.

Alessio, H. (1991). Use of educational games for difficult subject material, *Journal on Excellence in College Teaching, 2,* 71-76.

Ambron, J. (1988, November). Clustering: An interactive technique to enhance learning in biology, *JCST,* 122-127.

Boehrer, J., and Linsky, M. (1990). Teaching with cases: Learning to question. *New Directions for Teaching and Learning.* San Francisco: Jossey-Bass, 41-57.

Downs, J. (1989, Spring). Using thinkers' cards. *The Quick Fix, 37,* 61.

Fisch, L. (1986). Trigger films. *Innovation Abstracts, 8*(2).

Herr, K. (1989). Improving teaching and learning in large classes: A practical manual. Office of Instructional Services, Colorado State University, Fort Collins, CO.

Hughes, J. (1992). Approaches to teaching in the community college: What do faculty seek to accomplish? *Community/Junior College Quarterly*, 16, 189-197.

McKeachie, W., and others (1986). Teaching and learning in the college classroom. A review of the research literature. National Center for Research to Improve Postsecondary Teaching and Learning, Ann Arbor, MI.

Millis, B. (1990). Helping faculty build learning communities through cooperative groups. *To Improve the Academy: Resources for Student, Faculty, and Institutional Development, 10*, 43-58, Stillwater, OK: New Forums Press, Inc.

Schlenher, R., and Perry, C. (1986, March/April). Planning lectures that start, go, and end somewhere. *JCST*, 440-442.

Application and Integration

Education may be best defined, not in the context of transmission of knowledge and facts, but rather by the development of individuals' own active thinking abilities. Furthermore, what is knowledge to the instructor is only information to the student if he does not utilize it adequately or if his previous ways of understanding are not transformed (Erdynast, Romanoski, and McCormick, 1988). Methodologies to achieve this development are defined in the concepts of Problem-based Learning, Critical Thinking, Integrated Learning, and Authentic Learning. Although the language and perspectives of these concepts differ, they share the goal of achieving student ownership and success in activities designed to engage higher order thinking. Fourteen complex thinking processes have been described: comparison, classification, structural analysis, supported induction, supported deduction, error analysis, constructing support, extending, decision making, investigation, system analysis, problems solving, experimental inquiry, and invention (Schnitzer, 1993). These aspects of the classroom experience can be viewed as the refinement of a life skill: making choices in which there is no clear cut option and the individual is required to create the appropriate option based on an analysis of the contributing factors. Educators, then, teach students to be educators of themselves.

Students' level of cognitive development is often described using the terminology *concrete thinking* and *formal thinking* as outlined below (Apple, et.al., 1976):

Concrete Thinking

Uses classification, conversation, serial ordering and one-to-one correspondence in relation to concrete items.

45

Needs step-by-step instructions to solve problems requiring lengthy or complicated procedures; standard ways to solve problems preferred.

Needs reference to familiar actions, objects, and observable characteristics.

Learns new material slowly; memorizes buzzwords, formulas, and phrases; has difficulty in making applications without teacher help.

May not be aware of reasoning strategies used.

Formal Thinking

Applies combinatorial, multiple classification, serial ordering, and proportional reasoning in relating abstract ideas.

Can plan a lengthy procedure with minimal instructions given the broad goals; may use new and different ways to solve problems.

Can reason with concepts, abstract characteristics, and theories, using symbols to express ideas; sees new possibilities and implications of the big picture.

Learns new material easily; can use many critical-thinking skills with ease.

Is often aware of reasoning strategies and can select different strategies should the need arise.

Research has shown that as many as 50 to 90 percent of college students cannot reason at the formal level. This is, they lack the skills to reason abstractly and think critically (Novak and Dettloff, 1989). Classroom assignments such as term papers, critiques, experiments, and case studies require critical thinking. Students frequently perform below our expectations on such assignments, with college seniors performing only marginally above freshman in studies that have looked at the depth of argument students offer in support of a position (Kurfiss, 1989). It is important that we use a variety of teaching techniques, throughout the learning experience, that provide concrete-thinking students with opportunities to develop and use formal, critical-thinking skills. At the same time we provide these opportunities for purposeful feedback and practice, we must continue to emphasize the importance of an abundant and organized knowledge base for valid reasoning and encourage students to examine their methods of obtaining that base. Since students frequently rely on rote memorization of new knowledge, it is largely unavailable to them for argumentation or problem solving.

Students Resist Authentic Problem Solving

In order to develop critical-thinking skills, students must be actively engaged in problematic situations and challenging tasks which lack clear answers and stimulate a search for new, higher levels of knowledge. Often, though, it is these very challenges which students most vocally protest or passively resist. For example, we assume problem solving is a practical critical-thinking exercise, but our experience as instructors is that students do not often think through a problem by defining the problem, recognizing the basis of the problem, and planning a solution. Rather, their approach often seeks to plug data into a formula or, when available, to check the solution and work backwards toward developing a means of reaching that solution. Many students are unskilled in authentic problem-solving strategies and lack the confidence to venture into the task so they rely on a formula or some other device with which they feel comfortable. We may foster this approach when we teach problem solving by working examples or discussing solutions. In other words, we know the process for identifying and working through a problem, but can we help students see this process? Many instructors teach these steps to problem solving, using examples to show how the steps are applied (Walters, 1989):

1. Recognizing that a problem exists
2. Representing the problem (i.e., verbally or numerically)
3. Planning a solution
4. Carrying out the plan
5. Evaluating the solution
6. Describing the learning gained from solving the problem

In addition to the resistance to challenging assignments and acceptance of increased responsibility, many have described a kind of learned helplessness as a reason why some students perform so poorly in problem-solving activities (Sullivan, 1986, and Belenky, et.al.,

1986). Repressed cultures create a sense of alienation and powerless-
ness that makes even simple problem-solving tasks seem foreign and
unapproachable. Belenky, et.al., in *Women's Ways of Knowing*, describe a female without "voice" that typifies many of the nontraditional students we may serve in higher education today. The critical
thinking skills of confrontation and impersonal probing are objection-
able to these students (Heller, 1987). It may be most important that we
help these students find that they have "voice," that the authority and
positions of others can be questioned, and that their mind is more than
a bank waiting for some authoritarian deposit of knowledge.

Cooperative Efforts at Integrated Learning

Since our goal is to help each student develop skills in critical
thinking and problem solving, opportunities for practice often focus
on the individual, and each student is evaluated for her own approach
and solutions. However, most problem solving in everyday life occurs
in groups. Individuals who have developed skill in critical thinking
and problem solving may perform poorly in group efforts. That is, they
are unable to apply appropriate processes within the group so that the
sum of group thought reflects the richness of the potential sum of the
individual contributions. Providing practice opportunities which require students to evaluate a problem through establishing group criteria, then making and justifying judgments based on the criteria, and,
finally, selecting the most desirable outcomes will promote the growth
of collaborative critical-thinking abilities (Morris, 1989). Attention is
paid to group structure and teaching group members to be attentive to
group dynamics (see Class Discussion). Five standards of authentic
instruction have been described: higher-order thinking, depth of
knowledge, connectedness to the world beyond the classroom, sub-
stantive conversation, and social support for student achievement
(Newmann and Wehlage, 1993). When these are applied in the classroom, the ability to use higher-level thinking is accomplished in a
practical cooperative setting, applicable to today's workplace.

Strategies for the Classroom

A class which sets as its goal the development of critical thought within the field will focus on three areas:

1. Expanding the knowledge base with instruction aimed at students' understanding rather than coverage and activities which place students in the position of sharing the burden of learning.
2. Exploring procedural knowledge within the field; that is, the understanding of how "experts" in the field reason, evaluate, and create new knowledge.
3. Challenging students' current beliefs about knowledge in the field by presenting intellectual challenges at a level just beyond students' current beliefs and examining issues in diverse and sometimes conflicting ways. Students are supported in this challenge as the instructor provides structure in the form of clear explanations, instructions, and outlines and frequent opportunities for class discussion and feedback where students feel free to express new ideas. Without the latter, students tend to feel they are evaluated on the basis of their opinion or position rather than the strength of their argument.

There is a diverse selection of classroom activities that support these three areas:

1. Structure class content around a central problem or critical question. You may pose the question to students at the beginning of the class session, providing time for student discussion in teams. These teams may offer a solution based on assigned readings and prior knowledge or determine what additional research is needed. Time is reserved at the end of class for sharing of information among teams and clarification of difficult concepts and extensions of the material led by the instructor.
2. Ask students to verbalize, orally or in writing, the methods and strategies they used in reaching a solution.
3. Ask students to describe the elements of a problem by creating a schematic or graphic representation such as concept maps, cluster maps, and Vee diagrams.

In these types of activities previously learned knowledge is rearranged, new connections are made, and new thoughts are generated.

- **Vee Diagrams** provide an overview of the entire problem-solving process and the relationships between the various process skills (Germann, 1991). In Vee diagrams a large boxy "V" is drawn. The left side of the V contains the verbalization of background knowledge and concepts relevant to the problem, while the right side represents the process of evaluating hypothetical solutions and drawing a generalized conclusion. Since newly created knowledge lies directly opposite existing knowledge, and problem-solving steps lie opposite relevant concepts, it is easy to check frequently that the problem-solving process is staying on target.

- **Concept Maps** arrange the relevant ideas in a hierarchial fashion with the most inclusive concept at the top and the more specific ones at the bottom. Linking words between the concepts describe the relationships between the two words (Germann, 1991, Novak, 1979; Roth, 1990). Concept maps allow instructors to discover misconceptions in students' thinking and lend themselves readily to group collaboration as students debate concepts' meanings and relationships.

- **Cluster Maps** are a visual representation of a nonlinear brainstorming process believed to access both right brain and left brain function. As described by Ambron (1988) the instructor-facilitated activity begins with students selecting a dominant or nucleus word for the topic. This is written and circled on the chalkboard. The students then call out any phrase or word evoked by the nucleus word. These are quickly written on the board without judging relevance or importance. When suggested words relate directly to the nucleus word, they are immediately circled and connected to the center circle by an arrow. If any of these words or phrases directly elicits another, the two are connected by an arrow, building a chain of associations in multiple directions.

You may ask students to write short essays from these visualization tools, providing them with another opportunity to rearrange knowledge. The visualizations might be completed by small groups of students with each student then submitting her own written interpretation to allow assessment of individual understanding.

4. To encourage authentic approaches to solving mathematical problems, assign students solutions instead of problems. That is, supply a solution and ask students to develop an appropriate problem or explain the steps involved in reaching that solution.

5. Ask student to describe a process or concept to different groups of people using appropriate language, level of understanding, and perspective (i.e., group of professionals in the field/lay public or patient/patient's family).

6. Introduce new units of course content with student-generated Task Analysis (Novak and Dettloff, 1989). Students first write a behavioral objective which articulates a specific measurable learning goal (see Establishing a Learning Set). The students, working in tandem with the instructor, at least initially, identify relevant prerequisite concepts, steps, and procedures needed to meet the objective. This analysis includes a hierarchy of the specific steps involved, starting with the simplest step and progressing to the most complex level. The student input identifies information they have never learned or have forgotten. Again, verbalization is a key component. Students are verbally representing discrete steps that otherwise we can only assume they are aware of.

7. Semester-long investigative projects may also stimulate development of critical-thinking skills. Concrete-thinking students are challenged as these projects demand them to pose questions, plan and conduct research, collect and select relevant information, analyze findings, pose new questions, summarize connections, and represent these findings to others.

8. Select reading assignments which exemplify accepted modes of reasoning and thinking in the field. (See Suggested Readings.) Students are generally not aware of the process for acquiring new knowledge and understanding in a specific discipline. For example, professors in the humanities ask students to analyze, make judgements, and give interpretations while the sciences emphasize dispassionate and objective exploration of the facts. Select reading assignments which exemplify accepted modes of reasoning and thinking in the field.

9. Short writing assignments give students the opportunity to reorganize and clarify new knowledge. Such assignments can be used for three purposes (Brent and Felder, 1992):

    a. Exploring initial attitudes, for example:
       - What have you heard about this course?
       - What are your feelings about starting it?
       - What grade do you expect to get in it?
       - What was it like when you first learned to... (use the computer, solve word problems, use the microscope)?

    b. Activating prior knowledge, for example:
       - Briefly summarize what you know about...
       - List seven questions or things that you don't know about...
       - For each question you list, indicate why it might be important to know the answer.

    c. Increasing the relevance of the subject, for example:
       - List situations in your life when you have had to (or when you might need to) use the knowledge you acquired in class today.

10. In-depth critical writing addresses unstated assumptions, aspects of the topic not taken into account, or unsubstantiated conclusions in a reading or lecture (Brent and Felder, 1992. For example:
    - Analyze and evaluate the chapter/article you just read (or lecture, speech, news editorial, etc.)
    - Write a one-paragraph (one-page, three-page) objective summary.
    - Formulate at least five critical questions.
    - Draw conclusions about the validity or invalidity of the point of view presented and present arguments in support of your case.
    - Outline a procedure you might follow (interviews, experiments, etc.) to determine the validity of your conclusions.

11. Use problem-based, realistic case studies and role plays as the framework upon which to build or apply class content. (See Variety of Methods.)

12. Observational and practical field work provide a means of integrating knowledge with practice and giving students a more

realistic knowledge base for decision making and problem solving.

13. Have students design lab experiments. Give students a list of materials and pose a question which can be answered by experimentation. Students must submit the procedure they plan to use to reach the answer.

14. Play a 20-question game. The instructor thinks of some concept or process and students must ask yes or no questions to find their way to the answer (Greene, 1991).

15. Teach students decision-making tools such as fishbone analysis, decision-making matrix (Schnitzer, 1993, and Iozzi and Bastardo, 1990) and provide opportunity for practice in matters concerning both course content and course structure.

References

Ambron, J. (1988, November). Clustering: An interactive technique to enhance learning in biology. *Journal of College Science Teaching,* 122-127.

Apple, M., et.al. (1976). Science Teaching and the Development of Reasoning (A Workshop). Lawrence Hall of Science, University of California, Berkeley.

Belenky, M. F., Clinchy, B. M., Goldberger, N. R., and Tarule, J. M. (1986). *Women's Ways of Knowing: The Development of Self, Voice, and Mind.* New York: Basic Books.

Brent, R. and Felder, R. (1992, Spring). Writing assignments - pathways to connections. *College Teaching, 41*(2), 43-47.

Erdynast, Ramanoski, and McCormick (1988). The study of adult developmental psychology as an experimental stimulus to adult development. *Proceedings, 6th An. Conf. on Nontraditional and Interdisciplinary Programs.* Virginia Beach, VA: George Mason University, 14-20.

Germann, P. (1991). Developing science process skills through directed inquiry. *The American Biology Teacher,* 53, 243-247.

Greene, J. (1991). Making students think. *The Teaching Professor, 5*(8), 1.

Heller, S. (1987). Ineffective teaching and fuzzy assignments. *Chronicle of Higher Education, 34*(14), A13-20.

Iozzi, L. A. and Bastardo, P. J. (1990). *Decisions for today and tomorrow.* Longmont, CO: Sopris West, Inc.

Kurfiss, J. (1989). Helping faculty foster students' critical thinking in the disciplines. *New Directions for Teaching and Learning.* San Francisco: Jossey-Bass, 41-50.

Morris, A. (1989). Critical thinking and collaborative learning. *Innovation Abstracts, 11*(22).

Newmann, F. M. and Wehlage, G. G. (1993, April). Five standards of authentic instruction. *Educational Leadership*, 8-12.

Novak, J. D. (1979). Meaningful reception learning as a basis for rational thinking. 1980 AETS yearbook: *The Psychology of Teaching for Thinking and Creativity.* Columbus, OH: ERIC Clearinghouse for Science, Mathematics, and Environmental Education.

Novak, J. A. and Detloff, J. M. (1989, September/October). Developing critical thinking skills in community college students. *Journal of College Science Teaching*, 22-25.

Roth, W. (1990). Map your way to a better lab. *The Science Teacher, 57*(4), 31-34.

Schnitzer, S. (1993, April). Designing an authentic assessment. *Educational Leadership*, 32-35.

Sullivan, A. (1986). Teaching critical thinking and valuing as basic skills. *Innovation Abstracts, 8*(12).

Walters, M. (1989). Enhancing skills critical thinking: Linear vs. volume learning. *Innovation Abstracts, 11*(14).

Suggested Reading

Brookfield, S. D. (1987). *Developing Critical Thinkers: Challenging Adults to Explore Alternative Ways of Thinking and Acting.* San Francisco: Jossey-Bass.

Clark, M. E. (1989). Ariadne's Thread: *The Search for New Modes of Thinking.* New York: St. Martin's Press.

Esteva, G. (1987). In S. H. Mendlovits and R. B. J. Walker (Eds.), *Towards a just world peace.* London: Butterworth, 280.

Hart, K. (1990). *Teaching thinking in college.* National Center for Research to Improve Postsecondary Teaching and Learning, Ann Arbor, MI. Report no. NCRIPTAL-R-7.

Kaplan, L. (1991). Teaching intellectual autonomy: the failure of the critical thinking movement. *Educational Theory, 41*(4), 361-70.

Kurfiss, J. G. (1988). *Critical Thinking: Theory Research, Practice, and Possibilities.* Washington, D C: Association for the Study of Higher Education.

Leuders, E.(1988, Spring). Beyond specialization, writing for readers. *National Forum.*

Livingston, P. (1988). Literary knowledge. *Humanistic inquiry and the philosophy of science.* NY: Cornell University Press.

Marsh, P. (Ed.).(1988). *Contesting the boundaries of liberal and professional education: The Syracuse experiment.* Syracuse, NY: Syracuse University Press.

Moore, C. A. and Kinach, B. M. (1988). Linking the liberal arts and the professions: An integrative and interdisciplinary model. *Proceedings, 6th An. Conf. on Non-traditional and Interdisciplinary Programs.* Virginia Beach, VA: George Mason University, 204-208.

Salmon, W.C. (1984). *Scientific explanation and the causal structure of the world.* Princeton, NJ: Princeton University Press.

Stanford, M. (1987). *The nature of historical knowledge.* New York, NY: Basil Blackwell, LTD.

Stark, J. S. and Lowther, M.A. (1988). *Strengthening the ties that bind: Integrating undergraduate liberal and professional study.* Report of the Professional Preparation Network. Ann Arbor, MI: University of Michigan.

Stevenson, D. (1988). The development of critical systems thinking. *Proceedings, 6th An. Conf. on Non-traditional and Interdisciplinary Programs.* Virginia Beach, VA: George Mason University, 451-455.

Thacker, J. (1990). Critical and creative thinking in the classroom. *ERS Spectrum, 8*(4), 28-31.

Wales, C. E., Nardi, A. H., and Stager, R. A. (1986). *Professional decision making.* Morgantown, WV: University Center for Guided Design.

Wilcox, R. T. (1988). Teaching thinking while exploring educational controversies. *The Clearing House, 62,* 161-164

Wuff, D. and Nyquist, J. (1988). Using field methods as an instructional tool. In J. G. Kurfiss, L. Hilsen, S. Kahn, M. D. Sorcinelli, and R. Thiberius (Eds.), *To Improve the Academy,* Vol. 7. Stillwater, OK: POD/New Forums Press.

Classroom Evaluation & Assessment

Despite the amount of time spent measuring and evaluating student performance, it is a task most teachers dislike because the role of evaluator is perceived to be inconsistent with the role of teacher or helper. However, learning the process of evaluation and assessing the different types of evaluative tools will reinforce your role as teacher.

The Process of Evaluation

Let's assume that you plan to give a test over the first two chapters of your text. Even before you assign the chapters to be read, ask yourself two questions: "What do I want my students to learn from these two chapters?" "What should my students be able to do after reading these two chapters?" Using "Student will be able to" as your prefix, write your responses, being as *specific* as possible and using a measurable action verb. Note the following examples:

Student will be able to.....

(application) demonstrate three uses of a semicolon;

(knowledge) identify (list, define) three types of business ownership;

(knowledge) list four chief exports of Brazil;

(comprehension) summarize the front page story in the *NY Times;*

(synthesis) design an experiment;

(synthesis) design a brochure;

(synthesis) write a research paper;

(analysis) compare and contrast democracy and communism;

(evaluation) evaluate a poem;

(evaluation) edit a term paper;

(analysis) dissect a frog.

The words in parentheses indicate where the objective falls in Bloom's taxonomy for the cognitive domain. Once the objectives for the chapters have been identified, share these with the students so students know what they are expected to know and do, they know what the teacher considers "major" and "minor" points of the chapter, and they can predict probable test questions.

Once objectives have been devised and shared with students, the teacher must decide upon the best possible teaching methods and materials for ensuring students' mastery of the objectives. (See chapters on Methods and Materials.)

After the content has been delivered, the next step in the process is to evaluate for mastery of objectives. Many different kinds of evaluation are available:

1. *Canned Tests or Test Bank Tests*—Yes, they save time, but they range from good to awful, and frequently have never been tested in class (Langer, 1987). Too, a canned test cannot include your lecture material. Your test then implies that your supplemental content is unimportant. Students may, perhaps, have increased absenteeism if they know you test strictly from text material. In either case, exclusively using canned tests will seriously impair the validity of your course and your test.

2. *Teacher-made Objective Tests:*

   a. **Short answer and completion:**
      Advantages—easy to write and can ask many questions in a short period of time.
      Disadvantages—restricted to measuring lower-level learning.

   b. **True/False:**
      Advantages—easy to score, can be an effective way to measure factual knowledge as opposed to opinion, possible to ask many questions in a short period of time.
      Disadvantages—restricted to measuring the lowest-level of learning, may penalize divergent thinkers, may encourage guessing, and difficult to write items that are not trivial (Biehler & Snowman, 1993).

    c. **Matching:**
        Advantages—can cover much material in a small amount of space.
        Disadvantages—restricted to measuring lower-level learning, difficult to avoid irrelevant clues.
    d. **Multiple Choice:**
        Advantages—can measure many different levels of learning, opportunity for guessing is reduced, can ask many questions in a short period of time.
        Disadvantages—time-consuming and difficult to write items that measure more than just knowledge, may penalize divergent thinkers.

3. *Performance Tests*—Accountability has become the key word for reform in both public school education and in higher education. As a result, performance tests, those that measure how well students perform a particular skill under realistic conditions, have become an important evaluative tool for teachers to prove student mastery.

    a. **Portfolios**—as colleges move more toward an ability-based, outcome-oriented curriculum, portfolios are an ideal evaluative tool. For example, a history class portfolio might include a response to a lecture, an analytical essay, a column for the newspaper, a book review, an annotated bibliography. The actual selection of pieces and presentation of them is the responsibility of the student and allows the writer to be judged on work that is representative of the attained level in the course. The scoring or grading of the portfolio can be adjusted to meet any set of requirements (Winter & Winter, 1992). **Advantages**—frees the instructor to play the role of coach, makes student responsible for compiling portfolio, empowers the student as she selects or rejects projects for inclusion, reflects real-world writing, and is attractive to students who need more time to complete work (students with learning disabilities, non-native speakers). Last, but quite importantly, students know what they did at the end of a class and can feel a real sense of accomplishment for spent time, money, and effort (Winter & Winter, 1992). Denise St. Cyr (1993) says that the portfolio process extends beyond its academic value because students are distracted from working solely for a grade. They develop pride in their work as a master craftsman might.

   b. **Videotape**—using videotape as an assessment tool is not a new idea for athletic departments, but it is a relatively new idea for academic courses. Videotape can be used to assess a speech, oral reports, a presentation, mock trials, microteaching, inter-personal skills in small groups, a science experiment, a math problem-solving explanation, etc.

   c. **Hands-on Constructions or Projects**—maps, graphs, diagrams, lesson plans, scale replicas of architectural projects, physics projects, day-care center, a budget, accounting files, etc.

4. *Essay Tests*—Essay tests are a useful way to evaluate student comprehension and to encourage students to use critical thinking skills. Many teachers, however, hesitate to use essay tests because they feel that grading is too time-consuming and often arbitrary in setting standards of achievement. Following a few guidelines can help ameliorate this situation.

Guidelines:

   a. Take time to devise questions that relate to your objectives and word them so that students have a clear idea what is expected. Example objective: The student will be able to compare and contrast democracy and communism. Example essay: Compare and contrast democracy and communism, citing at least two similarities and five differences.

   If this essay question were given a point value of 21 points, each similarity and each difference could be worth three points each. Also, it is very important that the teacher write the prospective answer or at least an outline of the answer response, thereby foreseeing all possible answers. Grading becomes a simple matter once the question is exactly worded, the worth of the answer clearly established, and all possible answers delineated.

b. Philip Bishop (1990) suggests giving students possible test questions before the test to encourage re-studying of specific topics.

c. Another variation is to distribute essay questions at least a week before the test and suggest that students use them as study guides. On test day students are allowed to bring in one 3x5 card for all questions or one 3x5 card for each question, or a one-page note sheet for all questions. These notes enhance students' sense of control; too, they learn more because they reduced the content to notes.

5. *Tandem Testing*—this is obviously not a specific kind of test; it is a method and it is a motivator, but Julia Briggs (1990) has made it such an integral part of her course that it has actually become a kind of test for her. At the beginning of the semester, students form their own four-person study team. A week before an examination, student study teams are given study questions to review, and on test day, students are allowed to take the test in teams. Each student receives a copy of the test, but only one from each group will be turned in for grading. The one copy has on it the names of all persons on the team. Students may choose to take the test alone. Briggs reports the teams develop leadership skills, problem-solving skills, and teaching skills. They take ownership of the material and discover that teamwork pays off, that every member must contribute, and that camaraderie has a place in the college classroom.

6. *Collaborative Testing*—Barbara Walters-Bator (1987) also uses collaborative testing with her remedial algebra classes. Instead of a 4-person team, however, she advocates pairs. Walters-Bator allowed the students to sort themselves into pairs at the beginning of the semester. They studied together, worked together, and tested together, turning in one test with both names. As the semester continued, some partners

switched or went it alone if the pair was not working. Those who seldom attended or prepared for class were left to fend for themselves. Walters-Bator believes collaborative testing promotes individual growth and a sense of community which often leads to an enjoyment of mathematics, the ultimate reward.

C. Thus far, the focus has been on *summative* evaluation. Probably even more important than evaluation is *formative* assessment, or the monitoring of learning or progress in a non-graded way. Several assessment techniques are available to the teacher:

1. *Focused Listing (Cross and Angelo, 1988)*—Students list ideas that are critically related to an important course topic. Select a topic that has just been covered. Both students and teacher place the topic at the top of a piece of paper and list all the importantwords or concepts associated with that topic in a designated amount of time. Lists will be compared. This is an excellent opportunity to check understanding and progress.

2. *Directed Paraphrasing (Cross and Angelo, 1988)*—Select a point in the course after a major reading assignment or lecture. Determine an appropriate audience, time, and length and then have students paraphrase this important information. Separate the responses by labeling "confused," "minimal," "adequate," and "excellent." Give appropriate feedback and provide "excellent" models. This technique allows the teacher to find out quickly how well students have understood a lesson.

3. *Self-Diagnostic Learning Logs (Cross and Angelo, 1988)*—Much like a journal, students keep a record of each class or assignment. For each class, students make a list of main points they understood and a list of nebulous points. For assignments, students note errors as well as correct answers. On a regular basis, students analyze their successes and failures, their problems and successes, and summarize these findings. Logs should be collected and assessed regularly.

4. *One-Sentence Summaries*—An easy way to assess students' comprehension is to have them write a one-sentence summary of the day's lecture, reading assignment, etc., answering the

questions, "who, what, when, where, why, how?" Have students turn in the index card with their names on it at the end of class; it is also an expedient way to take attendance.

5. *Invented Dialogues* **(Cross and Angelo, 1988)**—This technique provides a creative way to assess students' understanding of the opinions and viewpoints of others in addition to clarifying their own. For example, perhaps a U. S. history class might create a dialog between an abolitionist and a slave-holder in the U. S. in 1855. Students could work in pairs, with each student assuming an opposing viewpoint.

6. *Assessment Cards*—Each student should fold a sheet of paper lengthwise. On the side of the folder paper, write T, F or any combination of 2-5 items for assessment purposes. For instance, if the teacher wanted to assess the understanding of Piaget's stage development theory, students might write "Sensorimotor," "Pre-Operational," "Concrete Operational," and "Formal Operational." The teacher could review characteristics of each stage, and students could "pinch" the correct response and hold up the paper. The teacher can assess understanding quickly, cover a significant amount of material at one time, and correct any misconceptions or misinformation on the spot without having to wait to discover this on a test. Everyone benefits.

7. *Student-Generated Quizzes*—Students bring to class a 5-question, short-answer quiz over the reading assignment. Quizzes are collected and then randomly redistributed and students take each others' quizzes. The writer of the quiz grades it and points out errors, etc. The teacher collects the graded quizzes and quickly assesses the level of comprehension by examining the responses and the questions.

8. *Compiling a Test Bank*—As part of the closure activity, students will collectively construct one test question based upon the most important information included in the day's lesson. A portion of the students' test bank questions will actually be incorporated into the next test. The teacher realizes quickly if the appropriate information was emphasized in the day's lesson, and the students are motivated to participate

actively with the incentive of "test" questions presented at the end of class.

9. *One-Minute Papers*—During the beginning of closure, students are asked to respond to two questions:

   a. What was the most important thing you learned in today's class?

   b. What question or questions do you have following today's class?

   c. Answers to these two questions are a quick, easy way to assess student comprehension (Cross and Angelo, 1988).

Planning the Test

Before an effective test can be constructed, clear and specific learning objectives must be in place. Many tests concentrate on the lowest levels of cognitive skills such as knowledge, the ability to remember and reproduce. As a result, higher order skills utilizing critical thinking skills are often neglected. As a rule, include some questions from all six categories of Bloom's Taxonomy, but make sure no more than 40% of test questions are knowledge oriented. Decide on the type of test items to use and write sufficient items to provide an adequate sample. After this is done, write a detailed key. A complete key reduces subjectivity and saves time later when grading or defending an answer.

During and after the grading process, analyze questions and answers in order to improve future exams. Classroom tests are frequently used as summative evaluations to grade students. They are not often used to provide feedback to both students and teachers on whether the learning objectives have been met. Formative feedback, however, can be invaluable to students and teacher because there is time to assess clarity of learning objectives and progress toward the mastery of objective and make necessary adjustments before summative evaluations are due.

References

Biehler, R., and Snowman, J. (1993). *Psychology applied to teaching.* Boston: Houghton Mifflin.

Bishop, P. (1990, February/March). Defining expectations: The essay test made simpler. Paper presented at the National Conference on Successful College Teaching, Orlando, FL.

Briggs, J. (1990). Why not team-testing? *Innovation Abstracts, 12*(7).

Cross, P., and Angelo, T. (1988). *Classroom assessment techniques. A handbook for faculty.* National Center for Research to Improve Postsecondary Teaching and Learning, Ann Arbor, MI.

Langer, P. (1987, Winter). Tips for teaching. *The Tutor.* University of Colorado at Boulder.

Roth, C. (1986). Tandem testing. *Innovation Abstracts, 8*(29).

St. Cyr, D. (1993). The portfolio process and accountability. *Innovation Abstracts, 15*(2).

Walters-Bator, B. (1987). The partnership exam. *Innovative Abstracts, 9*(12).

Winter, J., and Winter, E. (1992, March). Using the portfolio approach in teaching intercultural business communication. Paper presented at the Annual Eastern Michigan University Conference on Languages and Communication for World Business and the Professions, Ypsilanti, MI.

Suggested Reading

Abrami, P. C. (1985, Spring). Dimension of effective college instruction. *Review of Higher Education, 8*(3), 211-228.

Astin, A. W. (1985). *Achieving education excellence.* San Francisco: Jossey-Bass.

Blackburn, R. T., Lawrence, J. H., Ross, S., Okoloko, V. P., Meiland, R., Bieber, J. P., and Street, T. (1986, September). *Faculty as key resource: A review of the research literature.* Ann Arbor, MI: University of Michigan, National Center for Research to Improve Postsecondary Teaching and Learning.

Bloom, B. S. (Ed.).(1956). *Taxonomy of educational objectives: The classification of educational goals. Handbook I: Cognitive Domain.* New York: McKay.

Chipman, S. F., Segal, J. W., and Glaser, R. W. (Eds.).(1985). *Thinking and learning skills,* Volume 2. Research and open questions. Hillsdale, NJ: Lawrence Erlbaum.

Cranton, P. A., and Smith, R. A. (1986, Spring). A new look at the effect of course characteristics on student ratings of instruction. *American Educational Research Journal, 23*(1), 117-128.

Cunningham, P. M., and Cunningham, J. W. (1987, February). Content area reading-writing lessons. *The Reading Teacher, 40,* 506-512.

Gleason, M. (1986, February). Getting a perspective on student evaluation. *AAHE Bulletin, 38,* 10-13.

Henry, L. H. (1986). Clustering: Writing (and learning) about economics. *College Teaching, 34*(3), 89-93.

Hirshfield, C. (1984). The classroom quality circle: A widening role for students. *Innovation Abstracts, 6*(12).

Kogut, L. S. (1984, Spring). Quality circles: A Japanese management technique for the classroom. *Improving College and University Teaching, 32*(2), 123-127.

McKeachie, W. J., Pintrich, P. R., Lin, Y., and Smith, D. A. F. (1986, September). *Teaching and learning in the college classroom: A review of the research literature.* Ann Arbor, MI: University of Michigan, National Center for Research to Improve Postsecondary Teaching and Learning.

McMullen-Pastrick, M., and Gleason, M. (1986). Examinations: Accentuating the positive. *College Teaching, 34*(4), 135-139.

Noval, J. C., and Gowin, D. B. (1984). *Learning how to learn.* New York: Cambridge University Press.

Pascarella, E. T. (1985). College environmental influences on learning and cognitive development: A critical review and synthesis. In J. C. Smart (Ed.), *Higher education: Handbook of theory and research,* I, 1-61. New York: Agathon Press.

Riegle, R. P., and Rhodes, D. M. (1986). Avoiding mixed metaphors of faculty evaluation. *College Teaching, 34*(4), 123-128.

Roxbury Community College (1986, May). *Teaching from strengths conference..* Boston, MA: Roxbury Community College.

Schon, D. (1986). *Educating the reflective practitioner.* San Francisco: Jossey-Bass.

Segal, J. W, Chipman, S. F., and Glaser, R. (Eds.).(1985). *Thinking and learning skills. Volume I: Relating instruction to research.* Hillsdale, NJ: Lawrence Erlbaum.

Selfe, C. L., and Arbabi, F. (1986). Writing to learn: Engineering student journals. In A. Young and T. Fulwiler (Eds.), *Writing across the disciplines: Research into practice.* Upper Montclair, NJ: Boynton/Cook.

Selfe, C. L., Petersen, B. T., and Nahrgang, C. L. (1986). Journal writing in mathematics. In A. Young & T. Fulwiler (Eds.), *Writing across the disciplines: Research into practice.* Upper Montclair, NJ: Boynton/Cook.

Weaver, R. L., and Cotrell, H. W. (1985, Fall/Winter). Mental aerobics: The half-sheet response. *Innovative Higher Education,* 10, 23-31.

Weinstein, C., and Mayer, R. (1986). The teaching of learning strategies. In M. C. Wittrock (Ed.), *Handbook of research on teaching,* 315-327.

Willingham, W. W., with the assistance of Young, J. W., and Morris, M. M. (1985). *Success in college: The role of personal qualities and academic abilities.* New York: College Entrance Examination Board.

Wilson, R. C. (1986, March/April). Improving faculty teaching: Effective use of student evaluations and consultants. *Journal of Higher Education, 57*(2), 196-211.

Young, A., and Fulwiler, T. (Eds.).(1986). *Writing across the disciplines: Research into practice.* Upper Montclair, NJ: Boynton/Cook.

Zeiders, B. B., & Sivak, M. (1985, November). Quality circles from A to Z: King Arthur to Theory Z. *The Clearing House, 59*(4), 123-124.

Interpersonal Relations

Interpersonal relations is the ability to relate to students in a positive way which promotes a spirit of harmony and trust between student and teacher. Without this atmosphere of harmony and trust, the classroom environment may be a negative one whereby the teacher and students may be in conflict; it may be a fearful one whereby students are afraid to discuss or question for fear of humiliation, ridicule, or retribution; or it may be an indifferent one whereby neither party cares enough to feel anything at all.

Good interpersonal relations are essential for effective learning, so essential in fact that Jordon (1982) conducted research on the importance of the performance element in college teaching and discovered that professors' knowledge of subject was not as overwhelmingly important to students as most faculty assume; personal elements outweighed knowledge of subject. Some teachers seem able to develop positive interpersonal relations without even trying; however, other teachers must work toward that achievement. Kay Herr (1989) presents the following suggestions for improving interpersonal relations:

1. Let students know you care enough to learn their names.
2. Be aware of students' humanness.
3. Construct an atmosphere comfortable for students to contribute orally.
4. Use creative seating so students have the opportunity to get to know one another.
5. Go early to class to chat informally.
6. Let your excitement and interest about your discipline show.
7. Whenever possible, show where material is applicable to another course or area of knowledge.

8. Be available to meet with students outside of class during estab-
    lished office hours. If hours are changed or cancelled, place a note
    on the door.
9. Be aware of interests and background preparation of students.
    Have students fill out an information index card the first day of
    class. Sometimes tidbits of information from these forms can be
    worked into lecture.
10. Use humor where it is natural, spontaneous, and appropriate.
    Humor, of course, should never be sexist, in bad taste, or demean-
    ing to any student or group of students.
11. Have an individual conference with each student, either regarding
    a project, professional concern, or classroom activity.
12. Take advantage of the relationships already established. You may
    already know some of the students. If so, make casual remarks
    before and after class. Showing a good rapport with one student
    in the class will have a positive effect on other students.
13. Consider almost any comment worthy of your thought and re-
    sponse.
14. Be alert to changes in student performance. If a student starts
    performing poorly, make an appointment with the student to
    ascertain the reason. On the other hand, if a student's performance
    improves, congratulate and encourage the student. Let students
    know you are aware of them as individuals and that you care about
    their class performance.
15. Always treat students with respect.

Carolyn Mamchur (1989) says making a personal connection is a
key element in improving interpersonal relations. She states that
telling a story can show who the teacher is, it can illustrate many points
clearly, and it lets the students laugh at the human frailty we all share.
Another skill Mamchur(1989) feels is important to good interpersonal
relations is empowering students by providing sufficient wait time for
student response. She suggests that teachers ask a question, wait three
to five seconds before calling on someone, and then wait another three
to five seconds after the student stops speaking. Many times teachers
think a student has completed a response, when in actuality the student
was clarifying her thinking before continuing with the response.

Bob Magnen (1989) in his *147 Practical Tips for Teaching Professors* feels the first day of class is instrumental in establishing positive interpersonal relations. For example, he suggests that the teacher distribute the syllabus and give the students time to read it. Next, the class is divided into groups of three to five, and the groups come up with questions which would inform them about the class or the teacher, whether professional or personal. Next, they select a group representative to ask the questions. Many of the questions will be about the obvious—grading, assignments, attendance. However, some questions may concern qualifications to teach the course, experience besides teaching, hobbies. This type of interview allows the teacher to interact in a personal way—a positive first step in good classroom rapport.

Other suggestions Magnen (1989) has for promoting positive interpersonal relations include the following:

1. *Be a facilitator*—listen to students, question them, pay attention to their needs and interests. Many times students are poorly prepared—they can't use the library properly, they can't organize adequately, they can't read well, etc. Help them. Direct them to resources, give them suggestions and guidance, challenge them to develop.

2. *Be a socializing agent*—you are a representative of your field, especially the values, assumptions, and intellectual style that characterize that particular "micro-society." Socialize your students to the norms, standards, procedures, activities, and interests of your field.

Most students want to cooperate, want to participate, want to please; however, should they not, the onus is indeed on the teacher to establish positive relations. The student is our customer; therefore, our goal as faculty is to improve continuously our methods, materials, and delivery in order to keep our customer satisfied.

References

Herr, K. (1989). *Improving teaching and learning in large classes: A practical manual.* Office of Instructional Services: Colorado State University, 24-27.

Jordan, J. R. (1982). The professor as communicator. *Improving College and University Teaching,* 30, 120-124

Magnen, B. (1989). *147 practical tips for teaching professors.* Madison: Magna Publications.

Mamchur, C. (1989). Connecting with your audience. *College Teaching,* 37, 46-48.

Rowe, M. (1986). Wait time: Slowing down may be a way of speeding up! *Journal of Teacher Education,* 43-50.

Suggested Reading

Baughman, M. D. (1979). Teaching with humor: A performing art. *Contemporary Education* 1.

Beach, L. R. (1968). *Student interaction and learning in small self-directed college groups.* Washington, DC: Department of Health, Education and Welfare.

DeLozier, M. W. (1979). The teacher as performer: The art of selling students on learning. *Contemporary Education,* I.

Dunkin, M. J., amd Barnes, J. (1986). Research on teaching in higher education. *Handbook of research on teaching* (3rd ed.). New York: Macmillan.

Eble, K. R. (1976). *The craft of teaching.* San Francisco: Jossey-Bass.

Goldschmid, M. L. (1971). The learning cell: An instructional innovation. *Learning and Development,* 2(5), 1-6.

Good, T. L., and Brophy, J. E. (1987). *Looking in classrooms.* New York: Harper & Row.

McKeachie, W. J. (1978). *Teaching tips.* Lexington, Massachusetts: D. C. Health and Co.

Perry, R. P. (1985). Instructor expressiveness: Implications for improving teaching. In J. G. Donald and A.M. Sullivan (Eds.), *Using research to improve teaching,* 35-51.

Purkey, W. W., and Novak, J. M. (1984). *Inviting school success.* Belmont, CA: Wadsworth.

Rubin, L. J. (1985). *Artistry in teaching.* New York: Random House.

Schon, D. A. (1983). *The reflective practitioner.* New York: Basic Books.

Schwartz, L. L. (1980). Criteria for effective university teaching. *Improving College and University Teaching,* 28(3), 120-123.

Timpson, W. M., and Tobin, D. N. (1982). Teaching as performing. Englewood Cliffs, NJ: Prentice-Hall.

Classroom Management

Classroom management refers to the performance of day-to-day administrative and leadership tasks that allow instruction to proceed smoothly and efficiently.

Just as an orchestra needs a conductor to synthesize all the diverse instruments into a cohesive unit functioning as a mutually dependent body, such is the job of the classroom teacher—to orchestrate, to establish, and to maintain an effective learning environment.

As an administrator, a teacher's first class meeting sets the management tone for the rest of the semester and affects student evaluations. The effective teacher does the following during the first class meeting:

1. Reviews a thorough, detailed syllabus with the class so they know what they are expected to do during the semester. Make sure students understand attendance policy, late work policy, and withdrawal policy. A detailed schedule which outlines test dates allows students to feel in control of their learning.

2. Shows confidence in self and students and is prepared. Facing a roomful of strange students can be intimidating for even the experienced teacher. Switch the focus of attention from yourself to the students and begin identifying them as individuals rather than a class.

For example, pass out 3x5 index cards. Each row should have a different color. Get students' names, addresses, phone numbers, major, hobbies, and future goal. Collect these. If you match the same color card to the same number of row (e.g., pink—first row; green—second row, etc.) for all your classes, learning names will be easy. Students will predictably take the same seat on successive days, so names are narrowed and thus more easily learned. Secondly, have students pair. One person shares one minute's worth of information about herself, including most interesting experience; then they switch, and the other partner shares for one minute. Once time is called, one partner introduces the other to the rest of the class sharing the most interesting experience. Include yourself in this activity. This allows for learning some names as well as building rapport with students.

Do not go over the syllabus and dismiss class early the first day. This action sends a negative message to students; plus you would be denying yourself a wonderful opportunity to allow your students to see that every day is important, and that you are thoroughly prepared for every class, even the first day.

3. Knows other "student essential" information such as bookstore hours, parking sticker information, price of the text, next ACT test date, fire drill information, etc. Sharing this type of information with your students lets them see you care about them holistically, not just as a student in your class.

4. Takes attendance that first day. This implies its importance whether or not you have an official attendance policy. Inquire about missing members. You may get some information, but more importantly you let them see you are already thinking of them as individuals as opposed to a collective body.

5. Runs through what students might expect on a daily basis—assignment posted on board, course objectives posted on board, handouts on table by door for easy access, placement on table for homework/assignments, etc.

6. Begins class work the first day with an instructional activity that can be completed quickly and successfully. Successfully is the key word. You want to instill confidence, interest, and desire to return (Snowman & Biehler, 1993).

7. Is professional but pleasant and tries to establish a businesslike but supportive classroom atmosphere (Snowman & Biehler, 1993).

Other administrative tasks important on a daily basis include the following:

1. Place assignments on board before class.

2. Place class objectives on the board before class.

3. Double-check lesson plan to ensure all necessary materials are available.
4. If using instructional equipment, make sure it works before class starts. Have VCR tape wound to correct starting point.
5. Be available a few minutes before class so students can ask questions or to chat informally with the quieter or more introverted students.
6. Begin promptly on time. This lets students know class time is valuable and that their time is valuable.
7. Start with an attention getter. Ideas include critical thinking word plexers such as:

$$
\begin{array}{lll}
 & \text{Fe} & \\
\text{Fe} \quad \text{OLD} \quad \text{Fe} & & \text{(Old Ironsides)} \\
 & \text{Fe} &
\end{array}
$$

or, d s a n s o h i w n g (dashing through the snow); cultural literacy tidbits disguised as trivia (For committing what crime was Prometheus doomed to having his liver pecked out on a daily basis? For stealing fire from the gods and giving it to man.); or a startling statistic (Did you know that in 1990 48% of Hopkins County, KY residents read at less than or not better than a 4th grade level?).
8. After an attention getter, immediately review the last class lesson and establish a learning set for the current lesson. (See Establishing a Learning Set.)
9. Involve everyone in the class. Try to use as many names as possible during class. (See Variety of Methods.)
10. Save the last five minutes of class for closure. (See Closure.)
11. Erase the board before leaving class.

Jacob Kounin (1970) in his book *Discipline and Group Management in the Classroom* outlined the following group management leadership tasks for effective teaching:
1. Show students you are "with it." Be aware of physical conditions of the classroom, bored or sleepy students, a dominating student, the introverted student, body language signifying frustration, anger, or skepticism. Probably the easiest way to "train yourself in

awareness" is to tape a few classes and then look for about 10 clues such as staring out window, talking to neighbor, tapping feet, yawning, loud sighing, rolling of eyes, fanning, and shivering. Then you can analyze the situation to determine your responsibility for any of these behaviors.

2. Strive to maintain smoothness and momentum in class activities. Effective teachers do not interrupt activities, do not flip-flop from one activity to another, do not comment on an unrelated aspect of classroom functioning during an activity, and do not dwell on trivial incidents. Each time students are interrupted, they may be distracted and find it difficult to get back on task.

3. Try to keep the whole class involved, even when working with individual students or groups. For example, if some students or one student is working a problem at the board, have all students do the same problem at their desks. Or, if asking a question, pause long enough after for *everyone* to think of a response, not just the few who are quick to answer.

4. Be aware of the ripple effect. Essentially, whatever you say or do to *one* student affects *all* the students, not just the one singled out.

5. Ensure there is little wasted time, confusion, or disruption. There is no substitute for a thorough, well-organized lesson plan. This alleviates wasted time and confusion. Too, it sends a strong message to the student that you are well prepared and as a result, you have a right to expect them to be as well.

6. Set a no-nonsense, work-oriented tone, but at the same time promote a relaxed and pleasant atmosphere.

7. Give clear directions, hold students accountable for completing assignments, and give frequent feedback.

Influence techniques for facilitating good classroom management might include:

1. Proximity Control—simply placing yourself near the uninvolved student, the group dominator, the off-task student will often be sufficient to "nudge" student into appropriate behavior.

2. Convey interest in the talker or the uninvolved by asking a genuine question.

3. Humor is probably one of the most effective techniques. Humming the *Jeopardy* wait tune to let students know in a good natured way that sufficient time has elapsed for activity is effective.

4. Program Restructuring—if the delivery method or instructional resources are not working, restructure. Keep flexibility as an option. For example, if the discussion of pros and cons of congressional term limits is not provoking interest, turn it into a debate.

5. Do not allow yourself to become involved in a confrontation. Calmly tell the student that this is not the time or place for this discussion, but that you would be happy to discuss it after class. *Immediately* pick up where you left off and continue class.

6. If you have to deal harshly with a student for whatever reason, re-establish rapport and "start fresh" as if the occurrence had never happened.

7. Take time to reflect after each class. Ask yourself, "What worked?" "What didn't work?" and "How could I improve today's class?'

References

Biehler, R., and Snowman, J. (1993). *Psychology applied to teaching.* Boston: Houghton Mifflin Co.

Kounin, J. S. (1970). *Discipline and group management in classrooms.* New York: Holt, Rinehart and Winston.

Suggested Reading

Imai, M. (1986). *Kaizen.* New York: Random House.

Walton, M. (1986). *The Deming management method.* New York: Putman Publishing.

Wantuck, K. (1989). *Just in time for America.* Milwaukee: Forum.

Student Diversity

Statistics reveal the changing demographics in society; as a result, the profile of the "average" college classroom has changed as well. "Who are our students?" and "How can we help them succeed?" seem to be the questions to answer.

Community college students are older, less white, one-third learning disabled, and predominately female. If we acknowledge the correctness of this profile, then we need to ask ourselves some tough questions:

1.   Does the current curriculum effectively serve our student population?
2.   Do our delivery methods and materials effectively serve our student population?
3.   Do our tests and testing procedures effectively serve our student population?

In trying to answer these questions, let's examine some particular characteristics of our diverse students.

Learning Disabled

PL 94-142, the Education for All Handicapped Children Act of 1975, defines a learning disability as the disorder in one or more of the basic psychological processes involved in understanding or in using spoken or written language. The question is no longer "How do I know if any of my students have a learning disability?" It is, more likely, "How many of my students have learning disabilities?" You may or may not be able to identify those students, but if you know that as many as one-third of your students possibly have a learning disability, then you can modify your curriculum, pedagogy, and testing to help accommodate these students. There are many types of disabili-

ties, but there seem to be some common characteristics for any of the disabilities. According to Dan Parreira (1989), characteristics include:
1. Writes poorly
2. Easily distracted
3. Forgets easily
4. Reads poorly
5. Is impulsive
6. Copies inaccurately
7. Spells consistently *inconsistently*
8. Can express self well orally
9. Has trouble with variant word meanings and figurative language
10. Has problems organizing time
11. Thoughts wander
12. Has word retrieval problems
13. Slow worker—accurate; or fast worker—inaccurate
14. Has trouble answering "yes or no" to questions
15. Makes literal interpretations
16. Demonstrates moodiness
17. Is disorganized
18. Usually very capable students once coping or modification mechanism is in place

Strategies for Helping the Learning Disabled

1. Organize the lesson. Display an outline of the lesson on the board or overhead. Display lesson's objectives on board and check off as completed.
2. Chunk. If you lecture, limit one chunk to 10 minutes. Stop, review notes, fill in outline on board before beginning another chunk.
3. Use active participation and pictorial displays as frequently as possible. Abstract ideas are difficult to grasp without concrete reinforcement.
4. Allow verbal presentations in lieu of written; verbal facility is usually far superior.
5. Often, colored transparencies placed over the pages of the text will prevent words from "dancing around."

6. Use colored paper for handouts and tests. Stark white seems to impede concentration.
7. Give both written and oral instructions for better understanding.
8. Avoid Scantron forms. It is often difficult to put the right answers in the right place.
9. Multiple-choice tests are often difficult because of the subtleties of the different choices.
10. Have available copies of the *Bad Speller's Dictionary*.
11. Color seems to help organize. Color-code when possible.
12. A neurological straight line facilitates learning. For example, instead of working with text to the side of the notebook, have the text or the worksheet *above* the notebook so the head does not turn from side to side.
13. Consider alternative testing such as an oral test, visual display, or taping. If that's impossible, please give extra time.
14. When material is printed on both sides, give students two copies of each page or Xerox the material so students will not have to flip pages back and forth.
15. Provide student with a blank card to assist in reading an exam.
16. Encourage the use of a tape recorder.

We can remove some of the obstacles our learning disabled students face; the results could mean the difference between failure or success.

Multiple Intelligences

In the past, intelligence was thought of as being facile in math and language. After all, IQ tests, college entrance tests, and achievement tests emphasized those areas. With the advent of Howard Gardner's theory of multiple intelligences, however, the definition of intelligence has changed. Gardner defines intelligence as the ability to solve a problem or create a product useful to at least one culture using one, two, or any combination of seven intelligences: linguistic, logical-mathematical, intrapersonal, interpersonal, spatial, musical, and bodily-kinesthetic (Gardner, 1983). If college teachers accept Gardner's theory, our objectives, methods, materials, and assessment must change to reflect this philosophy. For example, we cannot continue exclusively to lecture and give paper and pencil tests.

Characteristics of the seven intelligences: *(Gardner, 1983)*

1. *Linguistic* - enjoys reading, writing, listening; tells stories, re-members names, dates, trivia; spells accurately and easily; has a highly developed vocabulary; likes crossword puzzles or playing games; highly developed auditory skills.

2. *Logical-Mathematical* - explores patterns, categories, and rela-tionships; computes math problems quickly; enjoys using com-puters; can group, order, analyze, interpret, and predict data; uses reason to solve problems logically; likes strategy games such as chess; likes working on logical puzzles; experiments with difficult concepts to gain understanding.

3. *Intrapersonal* - deep awareness of inner feelings, strengths and weaknesses; sense of independence or a strong will and is self-di-rected; reacts with strong opinions when controversial topics are being discussed; prefers own private, inner world; likes to be alone to pursue personal interest, hobby, or project; deep sense of self-confidence; different drummer in style, dress, or general attitude; self-motivator or independent projects; intuitive ability.

4. *Spatial Intelligence* - thinks in images and pictures; likes to draw, paint, sculpt; reads maps, charts, and diagrams easily; likes jigsaw puzzles and mazes; daydreams.

5. *Musical Intelligence* - aware of a variety of sounds in the envi-ronment; enjoys music or plays a musical instrument; remembers melodies of songs; knows when music is off key; plays music when working or studying; collects music pieces; sings, hums; keeps rhythm to music.

6. *Interpersonal* - likes being with people; has many friends; social-izes in a variety of environments; communicates, organizes, ma-nipulates; learns through cooperative activities; family mediator; empathetic toward others' feelings.

7. *Bodily-Kinesthetic* - learns by moving, touching, acting; proc-esses knowledge through sensations; switches, moves, fidgets

when sitting; likes physical activities; accomplished athlete; skillful in fine and gross motor skills, likes to touch people when talking; skillful in crafts; likes manipulatives, role playing, sports, action-packed stories.

Because teachers tend to teach the way they learn best, six-sevenths of the students are excluded. With planning, all teachers can include all seven intelligences in their lessons—not on a daily basis, perhaps, but certainly a few times throughout the semester so all learning intelligences are addressed and affirmed as important.

Ways to incorporate the intelligences include:

1. First, administer a multiple-intelligence inventory to get an idea of the class composition (you can make your own or get one from your counseling office).
2. Next, brainstorm for ways to make *your* particular discipline more accessible to all the intelligences. Art, music, and models are wonderful alternative means for "covering the material." Gardner (1993) feels that the greatest enemy of understanding is coverage. As long as you are determined to cover everything, you actually ensure that most students are *not* going to understand. He says that teachers must take enough time to get students deeply involved in something so they can think about it in lots of different ways and apply it.

Multiculturalism

Most Americans identify with some ethnic group—Irish-American, Native Americans, German-Americans, Italian-Americans, African-Americans, Chinese Americans, Hispanic-Americans, to name a few. Students' ethnicity can affect student-student relationships, as well as student-teacher relationships. Christine Bennett (1990) identified five aspects of ethnicity which are potential sources of misunderstanding: verbal communication, nonverbal communication, orientation modes, social value patterns, and intellectual modes.

For instance, some cultures value outspokenness while others such as the Native American culture prefer working on ideas in private. A form of nonverbal communication that is highly valued by American culture is direct eye contact. Among certain Native American and Asian cultures, however, averting one's eyes is a sign of respect for the other person (Bennett, 1990).

American culture is very time-oriented. Being on time is a virtue. The ethnic cultures of Hispanic-Americans and Native Americans are not so time-bound and may find education governed by time constraints to be frustrating.

Two more American values are competition and individualism. Mexican-Americans, however, value cooperation and family loyalty—both of which are at odds with values found in colleges which tend to reflect society's values (Bennett, 1990).

Even types of knowledge may vary depending upon ethnic values. Bennett (1990) discovered that some groups place a higher value on spiritual knowledge rather than scientific or on practical knowledge rather than theoretical. Many African-Americans, Native-Americans and rural whites prefer auditory/oral learning to reading.

What is the significance for college faculty? The American "melting pot" idea is gone; in its place is a pluralistic society; in our classrooms is cultural diversity.

Suggestions for dealing with an ethnically diverse student population include:

1. Maintain high expectations of all students.
2. Peer tutoring is effective for cultures valuing cooperation and mentoring.
3. **Cooperative learning**—small groups of students who help each other master material will be motivated to learn, will establish interpersonal relationships, and will learn more (Slavin, 1991).
4. **Mastery Learning**—assumes most students an master the curriculum if given enough time. The content is organized into a sequence of short units, allows students to progress through the material at their own rate, provides corrective feedback, and allows students to relearn and retest on each unit until mastery is attained.

5. Providing opportunities for conversation and cultural exchange, establishing a risk-free environment, and resisting the temptation to make assumptions strictly based upon observation will help make your multi-cultural classroom a success.

6. Instructional strategies that create interest among Anglo students may be as simple as changing the seating arrangement, adding color to transparencies, or using role playing. These approaches, however, may intimidate or complicate the learning experiences for some minority students (Biehler and Snowman, 1986).

7. Interest is also linked to student perceptions of usefulness of the topic. In the multicultural classroom, these perceptions of usefulness vary (Biehler and Snowman, 1986). Anglo middle class students may be motivated not by the immediate usefulness, but rather by a deferred relevance such as potential help for passing a grad school qualifying exam. For Black and Hispanic students, however, deferred relevance may be insufficient motivation. They may need to see immediate application. Faculty must present multiple purposes for the course and topics.

Carol Jenkins and Deborah Bainer (1991) identified the following professor behaviors that tend to communicate respect for all students during classroom interactions:

1. Pay particular attention to classroom interaction patterns during the first few weeks of class, and make a special effort to draw minorities into discussion during that time.

2. Respond to minority and majority students in similar ways when they make comparable contributions to class discussion. Enlarge on their comments, credit comments to their author, and coach both minority and majority students to offer additional information or further thoughts.

3. Be careful to ask minority and majority students qualitatively similar questions, and give all students an equal amount of time to respond to a question.

4. Make eye contact with minority as well as majority students after asking a question to invite a response.

5. Assume an attentive posture when responding to questions from minorities or when listening to their comments.

6. Notice patterns of interruption to determine if minority students
    tend to be interrupted more than majority students. Intervene when
    communication patterns among students tend to shut out minori-
    ties (Hall, 1982).

A college with commitment to the academic success of diverse
students must modify and/or develop teaching skills that will provide
equal access to learning in the classroom and weave minority students
into the very fabric of the college (Jenkins and Bainer, 1991).

Gender

All faculty should ask themselves this question: "Do I disempower
and devalue women learners?" There is research indicating that teachers give qualitatively different evaluations and feedback to women
than are given to men (Butterwick, Collard, Gray, and Kastner, 1990).
Through teacher-learner interactions, differential patterns of social
constraints and privileges are experienced by women and men. Who
gets to talk, who interrupts, and whose comments are acknowledged
indicate to women learners that they must comply with formal rules
while men are often encouraged to dominate by being recognized for
their aggressive behavior (Kramerae and Treichler, 1990).

Age

Non-traditional students (students over the age of 25) comprise
approximately 31 percent of the nation's higher education enrollment
(Heck, 1992). Non-traditional students, whether male or female, have
special needs on a college campus:
1. Non-traditional students attend classes primarily at night or on
    weekends because they either work or are responsible for child
    care during the day. As a result, these students are usually ex-
    hausted. A two-hour, 45-minute class can be torture unless the
    class is chunked into about five different variations of about 15-30
    minutes each. For example, a 15-minute lecture, note-taking ses-
    sion could be followed by a 15-minute small group activity. This
    could be followed by a teacher demonstration, followed by a
    simulation activity. A quiz followed by an active learning/ma-

nipul- ative type of activity could round out a productive, engaging evening.

2. The fear and anxiety of returning to the education scene after a lengthy absence can be debilitating. Use activities which foster rapport among the students, use small groups for cooperative learning, and consider performance assessment for at least the first test to build confidence.

3. Most non-traditional students miss orientation and may need help in learning "how to do school." Before assigning a library project, arrange for a library orientation or take the students yourself. College libraries can be rather intimidating where computers, microfiche machines, etc., are the norm.

4. Time management concerns are very important.

5. **Lack of Study Skills** - faculty need to urge non-traditional students to take a study skills class or incorporate study skills into our classes.

6. **Lack of Ability to Manage Stress** - many non-traditional students "disappear" during the course of the semester, not bothering to officially drop. Many times it is because they have become overwhelmed and didn't know how to handle it or didn't know to whom to talk.

7. **Lack of Personal Goals** - many students' goal is to survive the day. Suggest they keep two lists—one for short-term goals, such as writing a complete poem or filling out a financial aid form; and another for long-term goals, such as getting an A in history, finishing the semester, making the dean's list. These could be posted on the refrigerator and marked off as they are accomplished.

8. **Lack of Mentors** - ideally, advisors would occupy this role, but realistically, advisors who have more than 20-25 advisees could not possibly have time to be mentors to all their advisees. One encouraging faculty member can often make the difference in a non-traditional student's academic success.

References

Bennett, C. (1990). Comprehensive multicultural education: *Theory and practice*. (2nd ed.) Boston: Allyn and Bacon.

Biehler, R. F., and Snowman, J. (1986). *Psychology applied to teaching*. Boston: Houghton-Mifflin.

Butterwick, S., Collard, S., Gray, J., and Kastner, A. (1990). Soul search and research. *Proceedings of the 1990 Canadian Association for the Study of Adult Education Conference*. Victoria, British Columbia, Canada: University of Victoria.

Cordoni, B. (1987). *Living with a learning disability*. Carbondale: Southern Illinois UP.

Gardner, H. (1983). *Frames of mind: The theory of multiple intelligences*. New York: Basic Books.

Gardner, H. (1993, April). On teaching for understanding: A conversation with Howard Gardner. *Educational Leadership*.

Gleason, M. M. (1988, Spring). Teaching study strategies. *Teaching Exceptional Children*, 52-57.

Hall, R. M. (1982). *The classroom climate: A chilly one for women? Project on the status and education of women*. Washington, DC: Association of American Colleges.

Heck, J. (1992). *Special needs of nontraditional students*. Prepared for the Center for Teaching and Learning at Western KU in Bowling Green, KY.

Jenkins, C. A., and Bainer, D. L. (1991). Common instructional problems in the multicultural classroom. *Journal on Excellence in College Teaching, 2*, 77-88.

Kramerae, C., and Treichler, P. (1990). Power relationships in the classroom. Gender in the classroom. *Power and Pedagogy*. Urbana: University of Illinois.

Martin, J. (1991). Removing the stumbling blocks: 25 ways to help our learning disabled college writers. *NCTE*, 283-89.

Perreira, D. (1984). *Enhancing written expression of the learning disabled*. The office of Special Services, Marist College, Poughkeepsie, NY.

Slavin, R. E. (1991). Synthesis of research on cooperative learning. *Education Leadership, 48*(5), 71-82.

Suggested Reading

Adler, B. (1988). *The student's memory book*. New York: Doubleday.

Alley, G., and Deshler, D. (1979). *Teaching the learning disabled adolescent: Strategies and methods*. Denver, CO: Love.

Anderman, R. C., and Williams, J. M. (1986). *Teaching test-taking and note-taking skills to learning disabled high school students*. Paper presented at the 68th Annual Convention of the Council for Exceptional Children, New Orleans, Louisiana, April 1.

Austin Community College Study Guide Series. (1989). *Academic Therapy, 24* , 329-363.

Bastropieri, M. A. (1988, Winter). Using the keyboard method. *Teaching Exceptional Children*, 4-8.

Beirne-Smith, M. (1989). A systematic approach for teaching note-taking skills to students with mild learning handicaps. *Academic Therapy, 24*, 425-437.

Benne, K. (1982). The significance of human conflict. In L. Porter and B. Mohr (Eds.), *Reading Book for Human Relations Training*. Arlington, VA: National Training Laboratories Institute.

Bos, C. S., and Vaughn, S. (1988). *Strategies for teaching students with learning and behavior problems*. Needham Height, MA: Allyn and Bacon.

Cannon, L. W.(1990). Fostering positive race, class, and gender dynamics in the classroom. *Women's Studies Quarterly, 18*(12), 126-134.

Choate, J. S., Bennett, T. Z., Enright, B. E., Miller, L. J., Poteet, J. A., and Rakes, T. A. (1987). *Assessing and programming basic curriculum skills*. Newton, MA: Allyn and Bacon.

Clark, E. L., Deshler, D. D., Schumaker, J. B., Alley, G. R., and Warner, M. M. (1984). Visual imagery and self-questioning: Strategies to improve comprehension of written material. *Journal of Learning Disabilities, 17*, 145-149.

Colligan, L. (1982). *Taking tests*. New York: Scholastic Book Services.

Cones, J. H., Janha, D., and Noonan, J. F.(1983) Exploring racial assumptions with faculty. In J. H. Cones, J. F. Noonan, and D. Janha (Eds.), *Teaching Minority Students*. New Directions for Teaching and Learning, 16. San Francisco: Jossey-Bass.

Cronin, M. E., and Currie, P. A. (1984). Study skills: A resource guide for practitioners. *Remedial and Special Education, 5*, 61-69.

Derr, A. M., and Peters, C. L (1986). The geometric organizer: A study technique. *Academic Therapy, 21*, 357-366.

Deshler, D. D., and Schumaker, J. D. (1986). Learning strategies: An instructional alternative for low-achieving adolescents. *Exceptional Children, 52*, 583-590.

Devine, T. G. (1981). *Teaching study skills*. Boston: Allyn and Bacon.

Ellis, A. (1984) Rational-emotive therapy. In R. J. Corsini (Ed.), *Current Psychotherapies*. Itasca, IL: Peacock.

Ellis, E. S., Sabournie, E. J., and Marshall, K. J. (1989). Teaching learning strategies to learning disabled students in postsecondary settings. *Academic Therapy, 24*, 491-501.

Forgan, H. W., and Mangrum, C. T. (1989). *Teaching content area reading skills*, (4th ed.). Columbus, OH: Merrill.

Fraenkel, J. R., Kane, F. T., and Wolf, A. (1990). *Civics, government, and citizenship*. Englewood Cliffs, NJ: Prentice Hall.

Gearheart, R. B., and Gearheart, C. J. (1989). *Learning disabilities*, (5th ed.). Columbus, OH: Merrill.

Giordano, G. (1982). Outlining techniques that help disabled readers. *Academic Therapy, 17*, 517-522.

Gleason, M. M. (1988, Spring). Teaching study strategies. *Teaching Exceptional Children*, 52-57.

Hallahan, D. P., Kauffman, J. M., and Lloyd, J. W. (1985). *Introduction to learning disabilities*, (2nd ed.). Englewood Cliffs, NJ: Prentice-Hall.

Hauer, M. G., Murray, R. C., Dantin, D. B., and Bolner, M. S. (1987). *Books, libraries, and research,* (3rd ed.). Dubuque, IA: Kendall/Hunt.

Hoover, J. J. (1988). *Teaching handicapped students study skills,* (2nd ed.). Lindale, TX: Hamilton Publications.

Hoover, J. J. (1989a). Implementing a study skills program in the classroom. *Academic Therapy, 24,* 471-476.

Hoover, J. J. (1989b). Study skills and the education of students with learning disabilities. *Journal of Learning Disabilities, 22,* 452-455.

Horton, S. V., Lovitt, T. C., Givens, A., and Nelson, R. (1989). Teaching social studies to high school students with academic handicaps in a mainstreamed setting: Effects of a computerized study guide. *Journal of Learning Disabilities, 22,* 102-107.

Janha, D.(1988) A report on a workshop design to help faculty explore their race-related assumptions and practices. In M. Adams and L. Marchesani (Eds.), *Racial and Cultural Diversity, Curricular Content, and Classroom Dynamics: A Manual for College Teachers.* Amherst: University of Massachusetts.

Katz, J.(1983) White faculty struggling with the effects of racism. In J. H. Cones, J. F. Noonan, and D. Janha (Eds.), *Teaching Minority Students.* New Directions in Teaching and Learning, 16. San Francisco: Jossey-Bass.

Keil, F. C.(1984). Mechanisms of cognitive development and the structure of knowledge. In R. J. Sternberg (Ed.), *Mechanisms of Cognitive Development.* New York: W. H. Freeman.

Kirk, S. A., and Chalfant, J. C. (1984). *Academic and developmental learning disabilities.* Denver, CO: Love.

Leal, L., and Rafoth, M. A. (1991). Memory strategy development: What teachers do makes a difference. *Prevention, 26,* 234-237.

Lee, P., and Alley, G. R. (1984). *Teaching junior high school LD students to use a test-taking strategy.* Research Report No. 38, Institute for Research in Learning Disabilities, University of Kansas.

Lenz, B. K., Alley, G. R., and Schumaker, J. B. (1987). Activating the inactive learner: Advance organizers in the secondary content classroom. *Learning Disability Quarterly, 10,* 53-67.

Lovitt, T. C. (1989). *Introduction to learning disabilities.* Needham Heights, MA: Allyn and Bacon.

Lovitt, L. C., and Horton, S. V. (1987). How to develop study guides. *Reading, Writing, and Learning Disabilities, 3,* 333-343.

Mandelbaum, L.H., and Wilson, R. (1989). Teaching listening skills in the special education classroom. *Academic Therapy, 24,* 449-459.

Mann, P. H., Suiter, P. A., and McClung, R. M. (1987). *Handbook in diagnostic-prescriptive teaching,* (3rd ed.). Newton, MA: Allyn and Bacon.

McKenzie, R. G. (1991). Developing study skills through cooperative learning activities. *Prevention, 16,* 227-229.

McLoughlin, J. A, and Lewis, R. B. (1986). *Assessing special students,* (2nd ed.). Columbus, OH: Merrill.

Mercer, C. D. (1991). *Students with learning disabilities,* (4th ed.). New York: Merrill.

Miller, J. B.(1976) *Toward a New Psychology of Women.* Boston: Beacon Press.

Noonan, J. F.(1988). Discussing racial topics in class. In M. Adams and L. Marchesani (Eds.), *Racial and Cultural Diversity, Curricular Content, and Classroom Dynamics: A Manual for College Teachers.* Amherst: University of Massachusetts.

Paige, R. M.(1986). Trainer competencies: The missing conceptual link in orientation. *International Journal of Intercultural Relations, 10*(2), 135-158.

Pavlak, S. A. (1985a). *Classroom activators for correcting specific reading problems.* West Nyack, NY: Parker.

Pavlak, S. A. (1985b). *Informal tests for diagnosing specific reading problems.* West Nyack, NY: Parker.

Pope, L. (1982). *Guidelines for teaching children with learning problems.* Brooklyn: BOOK-LAB.

Raimy, V. (1975). *Misunderstandings of the Sslf: Cognitive psychotherapy and the misconception hypothesis.* San Francisco: Jossey-Bass.

Robinson, H. A. (1978). *Teaching reading and study skills: The content areas,* (2nd ed.). Boston: Allyn and Bacon.

Rooney, K. J. (1989). Independent strategies for efficient study: A core approach. *Academic Therapy, 24,* 383-390.

Rothman, R. W., and Cohen, J. (1988). Teaching test taking skills. *Academic Therapy, 23,* 341-347.

Saski, J., Swicegood, P., and Carter, J. (1983). Note-taking formats for learning disabled adolescents. *Learning Disability Quarterly, 6,* 265-272.

Scheid, K. (1989). *Cognitive and metacognitive learning strategies—Their role in the education of special education students.* Columbus, OH: LINC Resources.

Schewel, R. (1989). Semantic mapping: A study skills strategy. *Academic Therapy, 24,* 439-447.

Schumaker, J. B., Deshler, D. D., Alley, G. R., Warner, M. M., and Denton, P. H. (1982). Multipass: A learning strategy for improving reading comprehension. *Learning Disability Quarterly, 5,* 295-304.

Scruggs, T. E., and Mastropieri, M. A. (1984). Improving memory for facts: The "keyword" method. *Academic Therapy, 20,* 159-165.

Scruggs, T. E., and Mastropieri, M. A. (1988). Are learning disabled students "testwise"? A review of recent research. *Learning Disabilities Focus, 3,* 87-97.

Sedita, J. (1989). *Landmark study skills guide.* Prides Crossing, MA: Landmark Foundation.

Shepherd, J. R. (1982). *The Houghton Mifflin study skills handbook.* Boston: Houghton Mifflin.

Shields, J. M., and Heron, T. E. (1989, Winter). Teaching organizational skills to students with learning disabilities. *Teaching Exceptional Children,* 8-13.

Slade, D. (1986). Developing foundations for organizational skills. *Academic Therapy, 21,* 261-166.

Smith, C. R. (1983). *Learning disabilities.* Needham Heights, MA: Allyn and Bacon.

Smith, D. D. (1989). *Teaching students with learning and behavior problems,* (2nd ed.). Englewood Cliffs, NJ: Prentice Hall.

Smith, T. E. C., and Dowdy, C. A. (1989). The role of study skills in the secondary curriculum. *Academic Therapy, 24,* 479-490.

Vogel, S. A. (1987). Issues and concerns in LD college programming. In D. J. Johnson and J. W. Blalock (Eds.), *Adults with learning disabilities.* Orlando, FL: Grune and Stratton.

Wallace, G., and Kauffman, J. M. (1986). *Teaching students with learning and behavior problems,* (2nd ed.). Columbus, OH: Merrill.

Wallace, G., and McLoughlin, J. A. (1988). *Learning disabilities: Concepts and characteristics* (3rd ed.) .Columbus, OH: Merrill.

Wehrung-Schaffner, L., and Sapona, R. H. (1990). May the FORCE by with you: A test preparation strategy for learning disabled adolescents. *Academic Therapy, 25,* 291-300.

Weinstein, C. E. Goetz, E. T., and Alexander, P. O.(1988). *Learning and study strategies.* San Diego, CA: Academic Press.

Weinstein, G.(1988). Design elements for intergroup awareness training.*Journal for Specialists in Group Work, 13*(2), 96-103.

Weinstein, G., and Obear, K. (1992). Bias issues in the classroom: Encounters with the teaching self. *Promoting Diversity in College Classrooms: Innovative Responses for the Curriculum, Faculty, and Institutions,* San Francisco: Jossey-Bass.

Wesson, C. L., and Keefe, M. (1989, Spring). Teaching library skills to students with mild and moderate handicaps. *Teaching Exceptional Children,* 29-31.

Wilkerson, M. B.(1992) Beyond the graveyard: Engaging faculty involvement. *Change, 24*(1), 59-63.

Wood, J. W., White, B. L., and Miederhoff, J. E. (1988). Note-taking for the mainstreamed student. *Academic Therapy, 24,* 107-112.

Zaharna, R. S.(1989). Self-shock: The double-binding challenge of identity. *International Journal of Intercultural Relations, 13*(4), 501-525.

Learning Environment

Learning environment refers to the physical, social, and intellectual characteristics of the classroom which affect meaningful learning.

Physical characteristics include seating, temperature, configuration of the actual room, noise level, instructional resources—any extrinsic classroom factor. Often, teachers are "stuck" with a classroom that is not conducive to learning such as one having a narrow structural configuration, a raised platform at the front of the room, or bolted-to-the-floor tables; if the teacher is truly "stuck" for lack of available classroom space, modify the existing deterrents. Suggestions for improving the physical characteristics of the room include the following:

1. Check out your classroom *before* the first week of school. Make sure the room has a pencil sharpener, a wastepaper can, a clock, erasers, chalk, windows that are not stuck shut, at least two left-hand desks, and an operable viewing screen. The absence of these seemingly "little" details often become major obstacles for students.

2. Bernadine Gilpin (1989) reminds teachers that looking at the back of heads is not the best way for people to learn. As a result, seating arrangement is a very important consideration. Creative seating could include a horseshoe shape, a circle, or pods of five students at tables scattered throughout the room. Realistically, however, many classrooms or class sizes do not lend themselves to these formations. Kay Herr (1989) maintains there are other options. For example, if desks are arranged in rows, have students move up a seat every class meeting; the person sitting in the front moves to the back and everyone else moves up. Herr (1989) contends that seating patterns are established by certain personalities and learning styles.

Changing seats can also change student responses to the instructor as well as to each other. This technique will establish different teacher/student, student/student relationships and break routine. Most important, it can lead to improved learning. Herr (1989) also suggests that the teacher change locale; the teacher could start class at the back of the room, and the students would turn their desks or chairs around. A teacher who circulates around the room can circumvent even the most stifling seating arrangement. If you have several more desks than students, have students move close together. If students are spread out, lack of rapport and a feeling of spiritlessness may prevail.

3. Regulating the classroom temperature for comfort must be a universal concern. "Second floor burns up while first floor freezes" is a common lament among teachers; it is also one of the most difficult to do anything about. Keep three or four extra sweaters in your office and offer them to students for use during the "freezing" times. This action at least allows your students to know you are sympathetic to the uncomfortable room temperature. Bringing a stack of hand-held fans to class during the "burning" season will reveal your interest and concern for their well-being. For both extreme conditions, keep students actively involved and participating to help keep their minds off the extreme room temperatures.

4. Noise outside the classroom filtering into your classroom is hard to control, but the noise level inside the classroom can be addressed. Talking among students can be distracting and irritating to both you and the other students if the occasion calls for quiet. Do not stop the lecture or demonstration; stare at the offender(s) until they understand, keep talking and move toward the offender(s), call on the offender(s) by asking for a response, or use humor to make your point ("I think my Miracle Ear needs adjusting—a buzz is interfering with my train of thought."). Too, sometimes the introverted student knows no other way to get the teacher's attention. Wishing to be heard by the teacher without having to suffer the attention of raising a hand or saying "Excuse me, but...," the introverted student will comment to another student with the intent of being heard and addressed by the teacher.

In that case, it is probably better to pick up on the question or comment and address it immediately.

Social characteristics also affect the efficacy of the learning environment. Chickering and Gamson (1987) feel that frequent student/faculty contact in and out of classes is the most important factor in creating a positive learning environment. Faculty concern helps students get through rough times. Too, knowing a few faculty members well encourages students and enhances student commitment. Many colleges use freshman seminars taught by senior faculty members to accomplish this purpose; however, for the smaller college, simply visiting the student lounge, attending some student-sponsored activities, or leaving the office door open while working can establish contacts between student and faculty. In the classroom, setting a friendly tone can make learning enjoyable, not stressful. Suggestions for in-class strategies include:

1. Promote collaborative teamwork, not competition in isolation (see Variety of Methods).
2. Use active learning techniques (see Variety of Methods). Students do not get to know other students or feel a part of a group by sitting in classes listening to teachers. They must talk about what they are learning, write about it, relate it to past experiences, and apply it to their daily lives.
3. Respect diverse talents and ways of learning (see Student Variability). Students must feel that their uniqueness is appreciated and regarded as an asset in the classroom, not as a detriment.
4. Maintain an environment in which risks can be taken and mistakes made without fear of humiliation.
5. Kuh (1991) says that a community is made up of thousands of small gestures that keep people together and communicate feelings of belonging. For example, a small gesture is an expression of interest in a student's welfare, the comment in the margin of an essay acknowledging a salient point, a word after class, the note written by hand as a word of congratulations, sympathy or encouragement. Even thanking the class for a particularly lively, interesting session is a small gesture. Small gestures, however, are often more influential and remembered than course content (Kuh, 1991).

6. Help the students to know each other. Feeling a part of a group prevents alienation and isolation. Learn names quickly and make frequent use of students' names. Use small groups and have a group spokesperson begin each group presentation with an introduction of group members to the rest of the class. Do paired interviews the first day of class and make that pair responsible for each other, using the buddy system. If one of the pair is absent, the other calls to inquire, shares notes, information and handouts.

7. Recognize that students are not immune from everyday life difficulties. Offer assistance to a student who gets sick or whose family gets sick. Students' cars do break down, and babysitters do cancel. They could use a kind or sympathetic word or action during these times.

8. Peer critiquing is often a valuable tool to promote group unity (Gilpin, 1989). As students read, proofread, discuss and critique other students' work, they are privy to the quality and content of others' work. They realize they "are all in the same boat," and this promotes a feeling of kinship with their classmates. Gilpin (1989) also reports that students who do not participate during the first two weeks of the semester will usually remain silent for the entire semester. This technique, then, can serve dual purposes: promoting a positive learning environment and promoting student participation.

9. Sheppard and Fleer (1990) found through the Pentecost study that the older, non-traditional students have years of life experiences and practical knowledge which they are eager to contribute to class discussions. Often, however, these students may dominate the class and intimidate and/or discourage traditional-age student participation. For promoting a positive learning environment, be aware that you may be unconsciously encouraging this domination by responding favorably, thus giving positive feedback to these students. If you do, you will have two problems: more domination from the non-traditional student and more resentment from the others. Try to provide equal opportunity for everyone to contribute and do not allow any one person or group to dominate the class.

Intellectual characteristics for promoting a positive learning environment include challenging students to maintain interest but not overwhelming them. Finding just the right degree of difficulty so that the class proceeds on an instructional level, but not on a frustration level or independent level, should be the goal. This is not to suggest that courses should be "watered" or "dummied down." This is to suggest that after the first criterion-referenced test, an item analysis of the test be compared to students' performance. Set your mastery standard. For example, you may use 80% mastery as instructional, 90-100% mastery as independent and below 80% as frustration. In other words, you have established that 80% mastery of all material for all students is desirable and/or acceptable. If more than 10% of your students perform at less than 80% mastery, you need to determine the reason. Is there a pattern to the number of missed answers? Two weeks later, without announcement, assess students' retention by a follow-up assessment using a different type of assessment. For example, if the first test consisted of objective T/F, multiple-choice items, use a short-answer assessment tool. You may discover students do better; if so, this is a fairly good indication that concepts were mastered, but the objective test did not correlate to students' style of learning, the test was invalid, or the test was unreliable. If, however, the students performed more poorly, perhaps inadequate attention was given to concepts, students relied on guessing, or students memorized isolated facts without attempting to use elaborate rehearsal to place information in long-term memory. If students are learning on their frustration level, the teacher needs to consider the following:

1. Supplement the text with other resources—films, speakers, trade-books, journal articles, library research, etc.
2. Teach elaborate rehearsal techniques such as concept mapping, mnemonic devices, precis writing, learning logs.
3. Have available outlines for each class period so students can see the relationship between major and minor points.
4. Require periodic oral or written summaries.
5. Teach Cornell Notetaking Methods.
6. Supply a study guide or, better yet, have students collaboratively construct one.
7. Teach a lesson on test-taking strategies.

If students are performing at the 90-100% mastery level, supplement the class material with a project, presentation, or research. Or, also, consider that you may be asking too many low-level taxonomy questions. If so, seek to include more application, analysis, synthesis, or evaluation questions.

Intellectual characteristics for promoting a positive learning environment also apply to the teacher. Beidler and Tong (1991) suggest that a committed teacher will constantly strive to "recharge mental batteries" by researching in order to share new findings and new insights with students. Anything less is to become a "counterfeit intellectual" (p. 64).

Teachers also need to believe and endorse expectancy value theory. In other words, teachers must believe all students can succeed. Of course, just believing is insufficient; teachers must convince students that their actions of coming to class and studying will produce results, that the results will produce rewards, and that the rewards will be valuable. Then, *everyone* expects to succeed, and that sets the tone of a positive learning environment (Hodges, 1986).

Last, if you really want to assess your learning environment, ask your students (Willis, 1990). After the students complete one full week of class, ask each student to write two or three sentences on how things went during the first week of class and sign his/her name to the comments. A maximum of five minutes should be spent, papers folded, and passed to the front. Willis suggests going through the very same process at the end of the second week and again at the end of the third. After that, students should be surveyed in the same way every third week. Willis reports that students had worthwhile comments to share about the learning environment, evaluation, delivery methods and the school in general in the privacy of a note. He found students felt free to share both the good news and the bad news which becomes a worthwhile means of assessment and correction.

A positive learning environment provides for a variety of learning experiences, is built on mutual respect between teacher and students, and provides for interaction between the teacher and the student both in and out of the classroom.

References

Beidler, P. G., and Tong, R. (1991). Love in the classroom. *Journal on Excellence in College Teaching*, 2, 53-70.

Chickering, A., and Gamson, Z. (1987, March). Seven principles for good practice in undergraduate education. *AAHF*, 3-7.

Gilpin, B. (1989). *Teaching college success to older students: An instructor's manual.* Portland: Practical Psychology Press, 2-42.

Herr, K. (1989). *Improving learning in large classes: A practical manual.* Office of Instructional Services, Colorado State University, Fort Collins.

Hodges, D. (1986). How to encourage despairing students and prevent them from disappearing. *Innovation Abstracts, 8(*14).

Kuh, G. D. (1991). Teaching and learning—after class. *Journal on Excellence in College Teaching*, 2, 35-51.

Sheppard, V. and Fleer, M. (1990, May). Faculty and student development on the mixed age campus. Paper presented at the annual conference on non-traditional and interdisciplinary programs, George Mason University, 55-61.

Willis, L. (1990). How are things going? *Innovation Abstracts, 8(*11).

Suggested Reading

Adelman, C. (1984). *Starting with students: Promising approaches in American higher education.* Washington, DC: National Institute of Education.

Astin, A. W. (1985). *Achieving educational excellence.* San Francisco: Jossey-Bass.

Beal, P. E., and Noel, L. (1980). *What works in student retention.* American College Testing Program.

Bouton, C., and Garth, R. Y. (1983). Learning in groups. *New Directions for Teaching and Learning, 14.* San Francisco: Jossey-Bass.

Bowen, H. R., and Schuster, J. H. (1986). *American professors: A national resource imperiled.* New York: Oxford University Press.

Boyer, C. M., and Ahlgren, A. (1987, July/August). Assessing undergraduates' patterns of credit distribution: Amount and specialization. *Journal of Higher Education, 58*(4).

Boyer, C. M., Ewell, P. T., Finney, J. E., and Mingle, J. R. (1987). Assessment and outcomes measurement—A view from the states: Highlights of a new ECS survey. *AAHE Bulletin, 39*(7), 8-12.

Boyer, E. L. (1987). College: The undergraduate experience in America. Princeton, NJ: Carnegie Foundation for the Advancement of Teaching.

Chickering, A. W., and Associates (1981). *The modern American college: Responding to the new realities of diverse students and a changing society.* San Francisco: Jossey-Bass.

Clark, B. R. (1989). The academic life: Small worlds, different worlds. *Educational Researcher, 18*(5), 4-8.

Claxton, C. S., and Ralston, Y. (1978). Learning styles: Their impacts on teaching and administration. *AAHE-ERIC/Higher Education, Research Report No. 10.* Washington, DC: American Association for Higher Education.

Cohen, E. G. (1986). *Designing groupwork: Strategies for the heterogeneous classroom.* New York: Teachers College Press.

Cross, K. P. (1986, March). Taking teaching seriously. Presentation at the Annual Meeting of the American Association for Higher Education.

Ewell, P. T. (1985). Assessment: What's it all about. *Change, 17*(6), 32-36.

Gaff, J. G. (1989). General education at decade's end: The need for a second wave of reform. *Change, 21*,11-19.

Gaff, J. G., and Gaff, S. S. (1981). Student-faculty relationships. In A. Chickering and Associates, *The modern American college.* San Francisco: Jossey-Bass.

Gamson, Z. F., and Associates. (1984). *Liberating education.* San Francisco: Jossey Bass.

Gardner, H. (1983). *Frames of mind: A theory of multiple intelligence.* New York: Basic Books.

Kolb, D. (1984). *Experiential learning.* New Jersey: Prentice Hall.

Kuh, G. D., Krehbiel, L. E., and MacKay, K. A. (1988). *Personal development and the college student experience.* Trenton, NJ: Department of Higher Education College Outcomes Project.

Kuh, G. D., Schuh, J. H., Whitt, E. J., Andreas, R. E., Lyons, J. W., Strange, C. C., Krehbiel, L. E., and MacKay, K. A. (1991). *Involving colleges: Successful approaches to fostering student learning and development outside the classroom.* San Francisco: Jossey-Bass.

Kuh, G. D., and Whitt, E. J. (1988). *The invisible tapestry: Culture in American colleges and universities.* AAHE-ERIC/Higher Education Research Report, No. 1. Washington, DC: American Association for Higher Education.

Kulik, J. A. (1982). Individualized systems of instruction. In Harold E. Mitzel (Ed.), *Encyclopedia of Educational Research, 2.* New York: The Free Press.

Lowman, J. (1984). *Mastering the techniques of teaching.* San Francisco: Jossey-Bass.

McKeachie, W. J. (1985). *Improving undergraduate education through faculty development.* San Francisco: Jossey-Bass.

Pascarella, E. T. (1980). Student-faculty informal contact and college outcomes. *Review of Educational Research, 50,* 545-595.

Pascarella, E. T., Terenzini, P. T., and Wolfe, I. M. (1986). Orientation to college and freshman year persistence/withdrawal decision. *Journal of Higher Education, 57,* 155-175.

Peterson, M. W., Jedamus, P., and Associates. (1981). *Improving academic management.* San Francisco: Jossey-Bass.

Prins, D. J. (1983). Student services and policies: An outdated privilege or a necessary part of higher education? *International Journal of Institutional Management in Higher Education, 7,* 149-156.

Richardson, R. C., Jr., Fisk, E. C., and Okun, M. A. (1983). *Literacy in the open access college*. San Francisco: Jossey-Bass.

Winter, D. G., McClelland, D. C., and Stewart, A. J (1981). *A new case for the liberal arts*. San Francisco: Jossey-Bass.

Value Context

Value context refers to the instructor's inclusion of opportunities for students to clarify and make decisions about value-laden issues within the subject matter of a course. Citing the study of Ebbinghaus in 1907, which showed that memorized knowledge disappears over time, Erdynast, Romanoski and McCormick (1988) conclude that it is of little value to achieve goals of teaching content or maximizing coverage since these are quickly lost. They propose that a more appropriate goal of higher education is in the learning of knowledge that makes a difference in how students think about factual and moral issues. This learning is a lasting change in students' structure of knowing and choice of values and provides a foundation for future development. It is this goal of integrating value context which has fueled the inclusion of interdisciplinary and cross-disciplinary courses in college and university teaching. However, if we accept that a worthy goal of the college experience is not only to develop in students a knowledge base and a mastery of skills but also an enhanced awareness of their own thought processes and personal value base, each course becomes a suitable training ground in that effort.

The Development of Value Orientation in College Students

As instructors, we may be well served by understanding students' own value context and anticipating their responses to value-oriented activities based on their level of development. Understanding William Perry's classification of the developmental stages of college students will help us interpret student responses based on their individual development and encourage those advances we see toward more sophisticated approaches. Such knowledge certainly can ease our frustration as we evaluate student work that represents narrow views and falls short of a thorough examination of value issues.

Cutietta (1990) describes Perry's stages and the appropriate teaching strategies to encourage development in each stage in the following manner:

1. *Dualism* is the stage in which most students operate in high school and bring to the college experience. These students define themselves clearly on one side or the other of issues. Alternative interpretations and multiple viewpoints are not readily appreciated. These students view learning as the task of studying the authorities that know the answers and completing enough homework, practice and study to have enough knowledge to become like the experts. These students expect classes and teachers to give them facts. They do not seek or desire independence in choice or completion of assignments. They may not only resist, but, in part, be unable to consider multiple views or solutions to a single issue. However, as instructors introduce to these students differing beliefs and attitudes, they encourage students' development in seeing that the world in not clear-cut. As they find themselves agreeing with attitudes and values new to them, they reevaluate their notion of absolutes.

2. *Multiplicity* is the stage then entered by those students willing to explore values and positions with which they are unfamiliar. Their work will reflect an appreciation of competing values and an acceptance of differing interpretations. Students in this stage will be much more accepting of and challenged by small group discussions and value-based assignments. They look to the instructor, not as the final authority, but for acceptance of their work and guidance with suggestions. They most often first see all answers as valid and equal. Everyone has a right to an opinion and no opinions can be called wrong. However, these students may begin to question that if everything is equally valid, how is it possible to make intelligent decisions. This leads them to the third stage of development.

3. *Relativism* is that position in which students not only appreciate a diversity of opinion but realize that one opinion may be better supported by evidence that they personally feel is important.

Knowledge is no longer seen as a quantity but as qualitative and made meaningful to them in relationship to their values. Though often this level is not reached in the undergraduate years, students operating in this stage of development are willing to take responsibility for learning a topic of interest to them and sharing that learning with others. They become more comfortable in expressing their values and offering reasons in support of them. Students in this stage of development have reported comments such as: "It's not enough for me to take what someone says or writes about as fact. I want to know why they have taken that position, how they got there"; "I enjoy challenging myself"; and, "I listen more, ask more questions, and I don't believe everything I see or hear" (Erdynast, Romanoski, and McCormick, 1988).

Teaching Strategies to Develop Personal Values

Rarely do students take a single course or courses which have the primary purpose of developing value awareness; rather, they refine their understanding of their value system through interactions with a variety of instructors in a variety of courses. There are classroom activities, specific to the course being taught which encourage student awareness of their values. These activities may include:
1. Listing of individual student goals for the course
2. Comparison of instructor goals with student goals
3. Generating a class list of topics of interest
4. Prioritizing topics of interest from the instructor's list of possible course topics
5. Creating a continuum of concepts or contributors to the field from "most significant to least significant"
6. Drawing a map of classroom interactions
7. Debating pros and cons of an issue
8. Role playing all sides of an issue
9. Identifying and weighing various components of a whole issue (i.e., creating a pie graph)
10. Problem solving using issues of classic human dilemmas
11. Problem solving using problems of contemporary impact (i.e., case studies)

Value Issues in the Subject Matter

Most fields contain inherent value and ethical issues which can be explored as a component of class study to enhance the students' understanding of the role of values in society as well as develop a fuller appreciation for the complexity of the subject. Several simple but deliberate strategies can be incorporated to explore course content from the viewpoint of these values and ethics.

1. Asking questions that call for comparison
2. Asking questions that call for contrast
3. Asking questions that call for the statement of one's opinion
4. Role playing in which students take another's perspective
5. Providing completion statements that require evaluative positions from students; e.g., "I agree with the stated position because..."
6. Listing or having students list pre- and post-course values

For example, students individually, in pairs, or in small groups, may be asked to identify the primary value of the day's assigned text or other reading and its relationship to course goals. Students may be asked to compare or contrast views of two or more authors and identify possible underlying values that might account for similarities or differences. Another value-oriented assignment asks students to select from a reading one quote or view expressed that they especially liked and one they disliked and explain why.

When introducing a new topic, the instructor may ask students to decide upon a number of truth statements (considered by them to be true of that topic) and challenge or defend those statements by independent research. Another teaching strategy asks students to sit in a particular area of the room representing their view or opinion regarding a particular issue and then work with other students in that area to answer the question, "Why have you chosen to sit where you are?" In a thought-provoking twist of this debate strategy, the instructor can ask students to assume the values of a particular character in a reading, a member of the opposite gender, or another racial, ethnic, socio-economic group, etc., in order to argue an issue from another value perspective (Frederick, 1981).

Promoting Objectivity in Value Context Activities

Value issues lend themselves to discussions in which students readily participate and are therefore attractive to instructors wishing to promote student involvement in the classroom. Educators, too, value opportunities to support the development of students. However, we often shy away from value-laden exercises in course content to avoid debates which function on strictly emotional levels. Students are not likely to examine critically their values when they have chosen a highly emotional basis for their position. Bredehoft (1991) describes a highly structured technique for achieving a more neutral examination of a value issue called the cooperative controversy technique. A cooperative controversy is defined as "a learning situation in which two opposing sides are clearly drawn over a single issue; nevertheless, learners placed on both sides of the issue cooperate to arrive at a conclusion." The steps of the cooperative controversy technique are described below.

Procedure in Implementing a Cooperative Controversy (Bredehoft, 1991)

Step Procedure

1. During the class period prior to the cooperative controversy, the instructor identifies the question and assigns readings that present both sides.
2. At the beginning of the class period, the instructor assigns every student to a small group (four to eight students). Half of each of the small groups is assigned to the pro side and half to the con side of the question. The class is now composed of multiple, balanced groups of four to eight students.
3. The instructor reviews group rules:
   a. everyone participates and stays on task
   b. no arguing, all opinions are honored
   c. no side conversations
   d. the leader respects self and others

4. Concurrently, all pro groups and all con groups collaborate by sharing data about the controversial issue.
5. The pro and con sides join and place their chairs in a circle. The pro side presents arguments supporting the question while each member of the con side records the pro arguments on his/her work sheet.
6. The con side in each group presents arguments against the question while the pro side records.
7. Pro and con sides in each small group switch positions.
8. A second strategy planning session occurs.
9. The new pro side presents arguments in support of the question, and the con side records.
10. The new side presents arguments against the question and the pro side records.

Value context can be readily built into the structure of the course and into the development of the course content areas. Attention paid to value context will allow an instructor to be involved in the stimulation of the intellectual development of individual students and, therein, perhaps fulfill more closely the goals of higher education.

References

Bredehoft, D. (1991). Cooperative controversies in the classroom. *College Teaching, 39*(3), 122-25.

Cutietta, Roberta A. (1990). Adapt your teaching style to your students. *Music Educators Journal 76*(6), 31-36.

Erdynast, A., Romanoski, R., and McCormick, D. (1988). The study of adult development psychology as an experimental stimulus to adult development. *Proceedings: 6th An. Conf. on Non-traditional and Interdisciplinary Programs.* Virginia Beach, VA: George Mason University, 14-20.

Frederick, P. (1981). The dreaded discussion: Ten ways to start. *Improving College and University Teaching*, 29, 109-114.

Suggested Reading

Boyer, E. L. (1986). College: The Undergraduate Experience in America. New York: Harper and Row.

Daloz, L. A. (1986). *Effective teaching and mentoring: Realizing the transformational power of adult learning experiences.* San Francisco: Jossey-Bass.

Feletti, G., and Wilkerson, L. (1989, Spring). Problem-based learning: One approach to increasing student participation. *New Directions for Teaching and Learning*. San Francisco: Jossey-Bass, 51-60.

Frederick, P. (1989, Spring). Involving students more actively in the classroom. *New Directions for Teaching and Learning, 31-40.*

Johnson, D. W., and Johnson, R. T. (1986). *Learning together and alone* (2nd ed.). Englewood Cliffs, NJ: Prentice-Hall.

Kessler, D. J. (1988). How can we know Sacagawea? (Application of Value Context in American History). *Proceedings, 6th An. Conf. on Non-traditional and Interdisciplinary Programs*. Virginia Beach, VA: George Mason University, 263-272.

LaNoue, P. (1988). Linking campus issues with interdisciplinary studies curriculum design. *Proceedings, 6th An. Conf. on Non-traditional and Interdisciplinary Programs*. Virginia Beach, VA: George Mason University, 345-351.

Magnan, B. (1989). *147 Practical Tips for Teaching Professors*. Madison, W: Magna Publications.

McCollum, B. (1990). A pound of prevention: Integration of ethics into introductory accounting, *Innovation Abstracts, 12,* 23.

Perry, W. G. (1981). Cognitive and ethical growth: The making of meaning. The Modern American College. San Francisco: Jossey-Bass.

Sullivan, A. (1986). Teaching critical thinking and valuing as basic skills. *Innovation Abstracts, 8*(12).

Enthusiasm

Enthusiasm refers to the instructor's skill in communicating to students interest in the course content and in the students themselves. Mazzucca and Feldhusen (1977) found in a survey of students that teacher enthusiasm was particularly important to students, in both satisfaction with a particular class and in their own achievement in a particular class.

Although it helps to be energetic, expressive, and passionate, an instructor can still exhibit enthusiasm without those characteristics commonly associated with enthusiasm. In fact, enthusiasm can be conveyed in a number of behaviors.

1. *Seeking continuous improvement as a teacher.* Teachers who exhibit enthusiasm are constantly seeking "ways to do it better." Teachers might have students rate them every two weeks, using an anonymous 1-10 scale prefaced with a general comment, "On a scale of 1-10 with a 1 being the lowest and 10 the highest, rate me in response to Overall, how am I doing teaching this class'." Students will appreciate the opportunity to express an anonymous opinion, and teachers can gain valuable insight and show students they are indeed enthusiastic about their job and performance. As a follow-up activity of the rating, at the next class meeting the instructor can reveal the results and let the class know that anything below a 9 is personally unacceptable and ask for their suggestions for improvement. This should not take more than five minutes, and it can provide valuable feedback for teaching improvement as well as convey interest and concern in the students.

2. *Providing opportunities for active learning.* McKeachie (1994) suggests that one reason active learning is more efficient than passive learning may be the improved opportunities for feedback in active learning. Discussion provides the opportunity for stu-

dents to think and check their thinking against each other. A teacher who nods encouragement or smiles at the participant conveys interest and enthusiasm in students and the subject matter. Active learning activities, then, provide more opportunities for a teacher to reveal enthusiasm.

3. *Providing specific feedback.* Vague feedback such as "Good job," "Nice work," "needs improvement," is better than no feedback at all, but specific feedback conveys interest in student and subject matter, provides enough information to make a difference in future work, and enhances students' perceptions of their competence. (McKeachie, p. 365) Specific feedback includes comments such as "I can see the effort you put into this," "This sentence captures the mood of the story," "Good synthesis of observation and textbook material," "This project reveals much planning and organization." Specific feedback allows students to know the teacher thinks of them as individuals and worthy of the time and thought necessary for pertinent, individual feedback.

4. *Interacting with students outside the classroom.* Enthusiasm is conveyed when teachers take time or sacrifice time to help students out of the classroom. Tutoring, advising, or just listening over a cup of coffee communicates to the student interest and concern.

5. *Displaying positive non-verbal behaviors.* McKeachie (1994, p. 355) says that non-verbal methods communicate enthusiasm. He feels that facial expression, animation, and vocal intensity may be as important as the words teachers use.

6. *Displaying positive verbal behaviors.* Enthusiastic teachers make comments such as a) "We have a million things to do today."; b) "Is it time to leave already? We never have enough time."; c) "I just thought of an exciting idea. What do you think about this?"; d) "This information is extremely important, so I want you to understand it thoroughly."; e) "No one wants you to succeed more than I, for your success is my success."; f) "Let's change track for awhile. I notice some of you are looking tired and disengaged."; g) "Isn't that a fascinating piece of information. Do you get as excited as I when you read this research?"; h) "That is an insightful comment that needs some discussion. We don't have time right

this minute, so let's put it in our parking lot (draws circle on board and writes in topic for discussion), and we will address it at the end of class or at the beginning of our next class."

These types of comments reflect the following effective teacher behaviors:

a. Stresses major points
b. Maintains students' attention
c. Demonstrates interest in subject and its importance
d. Demonstrates concern for students
e. Feels responsible for student success
f. Uses humor and attention-getting examples
g. Stimulates thinking

Profile of an Enthusiastic Teacher

An enthusiastic teacher comes early to class in order to greet students and get objectives on board. An enthusiastic teacher is always prepared, has a detailed lesson plan, and has all necessary materials and equipment to ensure a productive class. An enthusiastic teacher uses a variety of classroom materials and methods and is always looking for ways to enrich, supplement, or "flavor" classroom presentations. An enthusiastic teacher never dismisses class early and expresses chagrin when class is over. He/she uses students' names often and freely, is available to students outside class, and tries to know something personal about each student so they have a basis for conversation beyond the classroom. An enthusiastic teacher never brings problems, complaints, or whining to class and expects a high level of performance from each student.

References

Cooper, J. (1990). *Classroom teaching skills.* .Boston: D. C. Heath and Co.

Mazzuca, S. andFeldhausen, J. (1977). *Effective college instruction: How students see it.* Paper presented at the annual meeting of the American Psychological Association, San Francisco.

McKeachie, W. and Others (1994). *Teaching Tips.* Lexington: D. C. Heath and Company, 282-283.

Suggested Reading

Abbott, R. D. (1990). Satisfaction with processes of collecting student opinions about instruction: A student perspective. *Journal of Educational Psychology, 82*, 201-206.

Aleamoni, L. M. (1978). The usefulness of student evaluations in improving college teaching. *Instructional Science, 7,* 95-105.

Bendig, A. W. (1955). Ability and personality characteristics of introductory psychology instructors rated competent and empathic by their students. *Journal of Educational Research, 48,* 705-709.

Benjamin, L. (1991). Personalization and active learning in the large introductory psychology class. *Teaching of Psychology, 18*(2), 68-74.

Cohen, P. A.(1981). Student ratings of instruction and student achievement: A meta-analysis of multisection validity studies. *Review of Educational Research, 51,* 281-309.

Leith, G. O. M. (1982). The influence of personality on learning to teach: Effects and delayed effects of microteaching. *Educational Review, 34*(3), 195-204.

Lowman, J.(1984). *Mastering the technique of teaching.* San Francisco: Jossey-Bass.

Marsh, H. W. (1982). SEEQ: A reliable, valid, and useful instrument for collecting students' evaluations of university teaching. *British Journal of Educational Psychology, 52,* 77-95.

McKeachie, W. J., Lin, Y-G., Milholland, J., and Isaacson, R. (1966). Student affiliation motives, teacher warmth, and academic achievement. *Journal of Personality and Social Psychology, 4,* 457-461.

Menges, R. J.(1990). Beliefs and behavior. *Teaching Excellence, 2*(6), 1-2.

Menges, R. J. and Mathis, B. C.(1988). *Key resources on teaching, learning, curriculum, and faculty development.* San Francisco: Jossey-Bass.

Menges, R. J., and Svinicki, M. D. (Eds.). (1991). College teaching from theory to practice. *New Directions for teaching and learning, 45.* San Francisco: Jossey-Bass.

Menges, R. J., and Weimer, M. G. (Eds.).(1994). *Better teaching and learning in college: Using scholarship to improve practice.* A publication of the National Center on Postsecondary Teaching, Learning, and Assessment. San Francisco: Jossey-Bass.

Classroom Discussion

Discussion engages students in the practice of inquiry within the discipline and allows them to develop skill in evaluating facts and drawing reliable conclusions (Clarke, 1988). Higher-level thinking is elicited during activities in which students have the opportunity to mentally manipulate and restructure conceptual information (Kealy and Witmer, 1991).

Discussion provides a means of assessing learning and providing feedback prior to formal evaluation tools. Students assess their own learning as they compare their understanding to that of their peers, and instructors have opportunity to provide feedback to students about shared misconceptions or successes and even identify individual students who may need additional learning opportunities (Wilkerson and Feletti, 1989).

The context of classroom discussion may include:

1. expanded student questioning techniques, where the instructor provides opportunities for students to elaborate upon their responses to questions;
2. teacher-centered discussions, where the instructor assumes responsibility for directing students' exploration of ideas; and,
3. student-centered discussions, in which the instructor's primary role is to facilitate and monitor interactions among students.

Promoting Discussion

Rarely does valuable discussion take place in the classroom spontaneously. Rather, to be successful, you must plan for student participation in discussion. You should give attention to several factors to ensure meaningful learning through discussion.

1. First, both you and your students should know how much and what kind of participation is desired.

2. Secondly, skill in asking questions at various cognitive levels enables you to guide students' consideration and exploration of ideas or issues.
3. Finally, skill in responding to students who make contributions or ask questions affects student participation.

(For a more detailed description of the types and functions of questions and appropriate teacher responses to student questions, please see Asking and Responding to Questions.)

A. *Suggestions for Structuring Class Discussion*

Clarke (1988) recommends initiating discussions with a guiding question on a transparency or handout that defines the problem and gives the students a chance to try initial responses. This is followed by a three-minute "free write" on the problem by each student which is used to begin the discussion. These strategies create a need to know on the part of the students and allows them to identify what they already know. You may wish to begin this activity with a short demonstration of the problem as it actually appears in a real setting through short film clips, newspaper articles, demonstrations, photos, case studies, or role plays. Following these initial activities, in-depth discussions may include time for students to search the text for factual evidence that supports their views.

To maintain the focused attention of the students, Frederick (1989) suggests for the instructor to think of the class session in 15-20-minute blocks of activity. These blocks include a minilecture on a new concept followed by an individual writing by students on a specific application or synthesis question with students then pairing off to explain their thinking to other students. The final ten to fifteen minutes of class are spent on discussing student responses. Based on these responses, the instructor provides closure and emphasizes important points. These writing components of the discussion plan aid students reluctant to readily share in discussion. They develop an ownership of ideas, have an investment in those ideas, and are ready to risk sharing them. The writing also slows down the quicker, competitive students who often quickly jump in and dominate the discussion, possibly with little forethought.

Often successful discussion is achieved when instructors merely rethink their expectations of class dynamics. While you will want to develop responses that encourage student participation, the key may lie in your level of comfort in silence. Typically, when students hesitate, the teacher talks; when the teacher talks, students assume a more passive role. Some think-time is necessary for students to contemplate the question and formulate their responses (Magnan, 1989). However, during the course of the discussion, there are several response behaviors that are likely to increase student contributions.

B. Response Behaviors that Promote Participation

1. *Simple Acknowledgement.* Simple verbal statements such as "I see what you mean," "Thank you," etc. No evaluation of the idea is given, but the student receives feedback that the idea has been heard.
2. *Praise.* Statements such as "good," "right," "that's interesting," etc. Praise may also be given to part of a student's contribution, such as when the instructor says, "Well, I'm not sure all of that is relevant, but what you said about the political implications is certainly worth considering."
3. *Restatement.* Repeating, rephrasing, modifying, clarifying, or expanding a student's idea are ways of recognizing an idea and emphasizing its importance.
4. *Probing.* Using questions which attempt to get students to re-phrase, clarify, or expand their ideas serves not only to let students know their ideas are worth pursuing, but also to elicit additional participation. Such questions should be designed so that you cannot anticipate the answer. Students are rarely motivated to critical thinking if it appears that the instructor is "fishing" for the desired answer. This can be achieved by prefacing questions with phrases such as "In your opinion why..." or "How can we accept..." (Herr, 1989).
5. *Redirecting.* Using questions which invite other students to clarify, expand, or comment upon a student's contribution encourages

a greater number of students to participate and to generate interaction among students.

6. *Acting Upon Students' Suggestions.* While opportunities to apply
students' ideas or to implement their suggestions may occur less
frequently, such direct action can be a powerful reinforcer. The
student knows that the idea is worth trying, and other students
recognize that their contributions will be taken seriously.

7. *Preventing Discussion Monopolies.* Sometimes student participation is limited because the instructor or a few students monop-
olize discussion time or direct the discussion toward areas of
specific interest. Cutting short such monologues or esoteric discussions may help facilitate participation from other students.

8. *Maintaining Direct Contact.* Students can be encouraged to respond to questions or comments when you engage in nonverbal
behaviors indicating interest and attention. Eye contact can be
used to encourage the individual response and to redirect students'
questions. Body movement and position in the classroom may also
affect student response levels and patterns.

In the booklet, *147 Practical Tips for Teaching Professors*, Magnan (1989) suggests the following strategy for helping students "visu-
alize" the discussion, reinforce the importance of student
contributions, and follow the natural flow of the discussion while
achieving the desired objectives. The topic is written on the middle of
a board or overhead with student responses and suggestions placed
around it, representing the natural flow of the discussion. While most
instructors feel more comfortable planning a set of prepared questions
to guide the discussion, this flow diagram will allow the instructor to
pick and choose questions in the order dictated by the discussion.

While these behaviors are likely to increase student participation,
it is true that this format maintains a "teacher-centered" classroom;
that is, the instructor assumes responsibility for leading students in
desired directions and maintains a high degree of involvement so that
most interactions will occur between the instructor and individual
students. In most cases, today's workplace requires students to acquire
skills in collaboration and group problem solving. This has motivated
instructors to search for ways to incorporate student experience in

group skills as they gain mastery of the academic content (Kealy and Witmer, 1991). In this strategy two types of learning occur—knowledge of concepts, principles and facts; and the procedures and social interactions required to use them (Wilkerson and Feletti, 1989).

Student-centered Discussion

In student-centered discussion and other group activities, the responsibility of the instructor shifts from tasks of initiating and directing discussion to providing an appropriate structure and assignment; teaching students productive group behavior and tasks; monitoring group function; and providing feedback and summary. While an instructor may not feel very involved in the classroom during group activities, the success and productive outcomes of those activities depend heavily on the instructor's prior planning and preparation and the degree to which both the instructor and students understand group dynamics.

The focus and structure of the group activity must be clearly communicated to the students. The suggestions for structuring group activity which follow this discussion provide a means for considering which kind of structure best fits a given task or desired outcome, procedures for initiating that activity, and possible pitfalls that may be experienced. You must decide upon and communicate to the students certain parameters of the assignment: what is the expected product of the group (a written summary, paper, list, etc.; or an oral report or sharing with other groups), whether this product will be graded or ungraded, and the time limit. You must also decide whether group members will be self-selected or assigned and, in classes where group work is an ongoing process, whether student groups will be maintained for the duration of part or all of the course, or reassigned frequently. Some regular practitioners of cooperative learning have found it useful to organize the classroom into teams at the beginning of the semester (Kealy and Witmer, 1991). Teams of about four are recommended. Some students will become passive in larger teams and smaller teams may not generate the variety of perspectives desired. In teacher-selected teams, attention should be given to providing for heterogeneity in achievement, sex, race, and age, as well as considering location of home, and interests.

If group activities are to be used extensively in the course, you may find it well worth the time and effort to initially teach students some of the fundamentals of team building and group dynamics. Team-building activities, as simple as deciding on a group name or logo, can accelerate the students' ability to work together and provide an atmosphere in which group tasks are accomplished easier and more efficiently. This instruction may also include a description of task behaviors and maintenance behaviors (Bradford, 1961).

Task Behaviors include behaviors engaged in by group members for the purpose of solving the problem or accomplishing the work which the group has undertaken.

Initiating: Offering new ideas relating to the group's task; suggesting how the group might begin to proceed, etc.

Information Seeking: Requesting factual or authoritative information relevant to the group's concern.

Opinion Seeking: Seeking clarification of opinions, beliefs, or values underlying suggestions made or relating to the task at hand.

Information Giving: Contributing facts or authoritative information relating to the group's concern.

Opinion Giving: Stating one's own beliefs, opinions, attitudes, values, etc., which are relevant to the group's concerns.

Orienting: Calling attention to group's stated goals and redirecting discussion when group departs from agreed directions or procedures.

Coordinating: Clarifying relationships among ideas and pulling ideas and suggestions together; coordinating activities or contributions of various members of group.

Maintenance Behaviors include behaviors engaged in by group members for the purpose of building unity and maintaining an atmosphere in which individuals feel free to contribute and communicate.

Gatekeeping: Attempting to keep communication channels open by facilitating and monitoring the participation of group members.

Encouraging: Accepting and supporting the contributions of group members, whether those contributions elicit agreement or disagreement.

Harmonizing: Attempting to mediate differences among group members or to resolve conflicts.

Energizing: Urging or stimulating the group to action.

A knowledge and awareness of these discussion behaviors may enhance the performance of the group. For example, discussion groups which never seem to accomplish anything because members frequently get side-tracked or go off in many directions may be suffering because no one performs "coordinating" behaviors; or, discussions which never get off the ground because nobody participates, may lack someone to perform "encouraging" behaviors.

Students today are very diverse in their experience and degree of comfort in discussion activities. Typically, students may think of discussion as opportunities to give information or opinions but are not aware of other discussion tasks and have given little or no thought to identifying the roles they feel most comfortable assuming. You may want to discuss these group behaviors and help students to experiment with various discussion roles.

Class discussion is not, then, an activity which is destined to succeed or fail with little that an instructor can do to influence its outcome. Rather, the instructor can contribute to improve interaction within the classroom by becoming more aware of effective task and maintenance behaviors; using and assisting students to use these behaviors; planning precise and thought-provoking questions and assignments; and, encouraging appropriate student contributions.

Classroom Assessment Techniques (CATS)

Classroom Assessment Techniques (CATS) (Angelo and Cross, 1993) can be very versatile tools for creating opportunities for student discussion in the classroom. Although CATS are often used as individualized activities they lend themselves to collaborative group work as well. CATS are attractive to instructors who deal with large amounts of content and are especially concerned with the time required to conduct certain discussion activities. CATS are quick and easy student-centered exercises which maintain a content reference, are derived from the instructor's objectives, and produce a measurable outcome. They can be, therefore, a good method of entrance into the area of classroom discussion for instructors who have not traditionally used these methods. Although several methods are given in the *Classroom Assessment Handbook* by Angelo and Cross, directions for four techniques which lend themselves readily to student group discussion are summarized here:

Focused Listing

1. Select a topic that the class has recently studied.
2. Set a time limit, a limit on the number of items, or both.
3. Ask student groups to make a list of important words, adhering to the limits, which describe the topic.
4. Students and instructor may review their lists and make additions or deletions as needed.

Directed Paraphrasing

Students are directed to work together in groups to paraphrase a reading or a lecture, using their own words, for a specific audience and purpose, and within a specific page-length or time limit.

One Minute Paper (Half-Sheet Response)

The teacher stops class a few minutes early and poses one or two questions to which students are asked to react. (Such as: "What was the most important thing you learned in today's class?" or "What question or questions regarding today's topic, remain unanswered for you?") The student groups can work together to write their reactions on half-sheets of paper or index cards the teacher has handed out. Five minutes should be given for this exercise.

RSQC2

The following description is taken from Angelo and Cross (1993).

R=Recall: Ask student groups to make a list consisting of a word or simple phrase, of the most important/interesting/difficult/useful points from the previous class session or reading assignment. (This should take 3-5 minutes.)

S=Solicit:

1. Quickly solicit the recalled information from the class, writing summary words or phrases on the board. Review the list, asking students to add any points they may see missing. (3-5 minutes)
2. Ask each group of students to choose from the revised list 3-5 main points and rank them in order of importance. (2-3 minutes)
3. Direct groups to then summarize the topic in one or two sentences which include all of their main points. (1-2 minutes)

Q=Questions: Ask student groups to jot down one or two questions that remain unanswered about this topic (1-2 minutes)

C2:

Comment: Invite the groups to write an evaluative comment about the class or reading; i.e., what I enjoyed most/least was...what I found most/least useful was... (2 minutes)

Connect: Ask groups to state in one or two sentences what they see as the connection(s) between the main point(s) of this assignment and the entire unit or course. (1-2 minutes)

NOTE: It is not necessary to go through all of the steps to benefit form the RSQC2 technique. Students may do only R and S or R, S, and Q with good results. After some initial experience with the technique, students may be asked to complete R as a homework assignment and complete S and Q in small groups in class.

Classroom Structures that Encourage Student Participation

(taken from Berqquist and Phillips, 1975)

METHOD	DEFINITION	WHEN USED	PREPARATION/PROCEDURE	LIMITATION
Buzz Groups	Allows for total participation by group members through small clusters of participants, followed by discussion of the entire group.	As a technique to get participation from every individual in the group. Highly adaptable to other group methods.	Prepare one or two questions on the subject to give each group. Divide the members into small clusters of four to six. A leader is chosen to record and report pertinent ideas discussed.	Thought must be given as to the purpose and organization of groups.
Symposium Discussion	A discussion in which the topic is broken into its various phrases; each part is presented by an expert or person well informed on that particular phrase, in a brief, concise speech.	When specific information is desired.	Leader meets with the three or four members of the symposium and plans outline. Participants are introduced and reports are given, group directs questions to proper symposium members, leader summarizes.	Can get off beam; personality of speakers may overshadow content; vocal speaker can monopolize program.
Debate Discussion	A pro and con discussion of a controversial issue. Objective is to convince the audience rather than display skill in attacking the opponent.	In discussing a controversial issue on which there are fairly definite opinions in the group on both sides to bring these differences out into the open in a friendly manner.	Divide the group into sides of pro and con. Each speaker should be limited to a predetermined time followed by a rebuttal if desired.	Members are often not objective towards the subject.
Experience Discussion	A small or large group discussion following a report on the main point of a book, article, movie, or life experience.	To present a new point of view or to present issues that will stimulate thought and discussion.	Plan with other participating on how review is to be presented. Then have an open discussion on pertinent issues and point of view as experienced.	Ability of participating members to relate to others and motivate thinking.

Concentric Circle	A small group of group members form within the larger circle. The inner circle discusses a topic while the role of the outside circle is to listen. The discussion is then reversed.	As a technique to stimulate interest and to provoke good discussion. This is especially good to get more response from a group that is slow in participating.	Leader and planning group work out questions that will be discussed by the concentric circle and then by the larger circle.	Much thought and preparation must be given to the questions for discussion. Room and movable chairs needed.
Reaction Sheet	A method of reacting to ideas in the following ways: Ideas that you question; ideas that are new to you; ideas that really "hit home."	As a way to get the group to react. Combine this with other methods.	Prepare topic and reaction sheet. Explain and distribute reaction sheets with the instructions to write as they listen, watch, or read. Follow with group discussion.	Topic should be somewhat controversial.
Phillips 66	This is a spontaneous method where six people view their opinions on a topic for six minutes.	To add spice and variety to methods of presentation.	Define topic of discussion. Count off six people and allow six minutes for discussion. Allow for group discussion or reassignment of six people.	Must be used somewhat flexibly.
Reverse Thinking	Expression of thought by thinking in reverse.	To gain an insight into others' feelings and to see another point of view.	Prepare topic—explain to group the theory of reverse thinking. Combine with other methods.	A challenge to group members.
Role Playing	The spontaneous acting out of a situation or an incident by selected members of the group.	As the basis of developing clearer insights into the feelings of people and the forces in a situation which facilitates or blocks good human relations.	Choose an appropriate situation or problem. Have the group define the roles—the general characteristics to be represented by each player. Observe and discuss such things as specific behavior, underlying forces, or emotional reactions.	Group leader must be skilled so that actors will play their roles seriously, without self-consciousness.

Picture Making	A way of bringing out ideas or principles on a topic by means of simple illustrations made by group members on the blackboard or large chart paper.	As a technique to stimulate interest, thinking, and participation.	Leader and members of planning group select general principles or questions on the topic which would be suitable to illustrate. Leader divides the group into four or five subgroups. Each subgroup is given a statement or problem to illustrate. After making, each group shows and explain the picture. This is followed by discussion.	Instruction must be clear as to the value of picture making and adequate materials supplies.
Brain Storming	Technique in creative thinking in which group members storm a problem with their brains.	To get new ideas, and release individual potentialities in thinking up ideas.	Leader and members of planning group select suitable problems or questions on the topic selected by the entire group. Procedure: The leader explains to the group the meaning of brainstorming and the following rules: Judicial (critical) judgments ruled out. Criticism to be applied later. Quantity of ideas wanted. The more ideas the better the chances of good ones. Free wheeling welcomed. The wilder the idea the better; it's easier to tame them down than to pump them up. Hitchhiking is legitimate. If you can improve someone else's ideas, so much better. Leader rings bell when one of the above rules is violated. Recorder lists the ideas. Follow-up—type list and bring to next meeting to give to members.	To be utilized as only a part of a class.

References

Angelo, T.A. and Cross, K. P. (1993). *Classroom Assessment Techniques: A Handbook for College Teachers* (2nd ed.). San Francisco: Jossey-Bass.

Berqquist, W. H. and Phillips, S. R. (1975). *A Handbook for Faculty Development, I,* Washington DC: The Council for the Advancement of Small Colleges.

Bradford, L. P. (Ed.).(1961). *Group Development.* Washington: National Training Laboratory, National Education Association.

Clarke, J. (1988, Fall). Designing discussion as group inquiry. *College Teaching ,* 140-143.

Erickson, B. (1977). Clinic to improve university teaching. University of Massachusetts at Amherst.

Frederick, P. (1989, Spring). Involving students more actively in the classroom. *New Directions for Teaching and Learning ,* 31-40.

Herr, K. (1989). *Improving teaching and learning in large classes: A practice manual.* Office of Instructional Services, Colorado State University.

Kealy, R., and Witmer, K. (1991). Cooperative learning in higher education: An alternative approach to collegiate instruction (unpublished).

Magnan, B. (1989). *147 Practical Tips for Teaching Professors.* Madison, WI: Magna Publications.

Wilkerson, L.A. and Feletti, G. (1989). Problem-based learning: One approach to increasing student participation. *New Directions in Teaching and Learning, 37.* San Francisco: Jossey-Bass.

Suggested Reading

Andre, T. (1986). *Cognitive Learning: Understanding, Thinking and Problem Solving.* New York: Academic Press.

Barrows, H. S., Meyers, A., Williams, R. G., and Moticka, E. J. (1986). Large-group problem-based learning: A possible solution for the 2 Sigma Problem. *Medical Teacher, 8,* 325-331.

Bonwell, C. C., and Eison, J. (1991). *Active learning creating excitement in the classroom.* ASHE-ERIC Higher Education Report No. 1. Washington, DC: The George Washington University, School of Education and Human Development.

Boud, D. (Ed.).(1986). *Problem-based learning in education for the professions.* Sidney: University of New South Wales.

Boyer, E. L. (1986). College: *The Undergraduate Experience in America.* New York: Harper and Row.

Chickering, A., and Gamson, Z. (1987). Seven principles for good practice in undergraduate education. *AAHE Bulletin, 39*(7), 3-7.

Christiansen, R. C., and Hansen, A. J. (1987). *Teaching and the Case Method.* Boston: Harvard Business School.

Clarke, J. (1987, Spring). Building a lecture that works. *College Teaching*, 35(2).

Cooper, J., and Mueck, R. (1989). Annotated bibliography of cooperative/collaborative learning: Research and practice (primarily) at the collegiate level. *Journal of Research and Development in Education.*

Cross, K. P. (1987). The adventures of education in wonderland:Implementing education reform. *Phi Delta Kappan*, 68(7), 498-499.

Cuseo, J. (1989). Cooperative learning: Why does it work? *Cooperative Learning and College Teaching*, 1, 3-8.

Feletti, G., and Wilkerson, L. (1989, Spring). Problem-based learning: One approach to increasing student participation. *New Directions for Teaching and Learning*, 51-60. San Francisco: Jossey-Bass.

Fong, B. (1987). Commonplaces about teaching: Second thoughts. *Change*, 19(4), 28-29.

Frederick, P. (1981). The dreaded discussion: Ten ways to start. *Improving College and University Teaching*, 29, 109-114.

Frederick, P. (1986). The lively lecture—Eight variations. *College Teaching*, 34(2), 43-50.

Frierson, H. (1986). Two intervention methods: Effects on groups of predominantly black nursing students' board scores. *Journal of Research and Development in Education*, 9, 18-23.

Fulwiler, T. (1987). *Teaching with Writing*. Upper Montclair, New Jersey: Boynton.

Johnson, D. W., and Johnson, R. T. (1986). *Learning Together and Alone*, (2nd ed.). Englewood Cliffs, NJ: Prentice-Hall.

Kagan, S. (1989). *Cooperative Learning: Resource for Teachers*. San Juan Capistrano, CA: Resources for Teachers.

McKeachie, W. (1986). *Teaching tips: A guidebook for the beginning teacher.*. Lexington, MA: Heath.

Sharan, S., and Shachar, C. (1988). *Language and Learning in the Cooperative Classroom*. New York: Springer Verlag.

Slavin, R. E. (1990). *Cooperative Learning: Theory, Research, and Practice*. Englewood Cliffs, NJ: Prentice Hall.

Webb, N. (1985). Student interaction and learning in small groups: A research summary, learning to cooperate, cooperating to learn. New York: Plenum.

Asking and Responding to Questions

Asking and responding to questions refers to the instructor's ability to use appropriate questions for instructional purposes and to answer questions clearly to promote understanding and participation.

John Dewey pointed out that thinking itself is questioning. He said (Dewey, 1933), "What's in a question, you ask? Everything. It is the way of evoking stimulating response or stultifying inquiry. It is, in essence, the very core of teaching" (p. 266).

Certainly, the importance of questions in the classroom is acknowledged, and the frequency of questions in the classroom is quite high (Gall, 1970). However, most of the questions asked are memory, calling for only a superficial understanding of the material (Gall, 1970). It appears, then, that instructors need to become more skillful at asking more higher-level, thought-provoking questions.

Types of Questions

Questions have distinct characteristics, serve various functions, and require different levels of thinking. Understanding Bloom's Taxonomy is an important first step in formulating good questions.

Levels of the Taxonomy

1. The first level, **knowledge**, requires the student to recall information, not manipulate it, but merely recall it the way it was learned. This level is important because students must have a base of knowledge before they can think at higher levels; however, this level is overused. Words often found in knowledge questions are *define, list, identify, who, what, where, when*. Examples: Who

wrote Hamlet? What states border Arizona? Define homeostasis.
List the five steps of the problem-solving model. When was
abortion legalized?

2. The second level, **comprehension**, requires that students take
   recall information and demonstrate a personal grasp of the material by being able to rephrase it. Words often found in comprehension questions are *summarize, describe, explain, compare,
   contrast.* Examples: Compare socialism and communism. Explain
   what the author suggests were the main reasons for the Civil War.
   Describe the chemical process resulting from this experiment.
   Summarize the last four chapters of *Grapes of Wrath.* Contrast
   Piaget's and Erikson's definition of "stage."

3. The third level, **application**, requires students to be able to apply
   previously learned information. Words often found in application
   questions are *solve, apply, classify, use, make, employ, which, how
   many, construct, write.* Examples: Solve this problem by using the
   procedure we discussed for quadratic equations. Write a lesson
   plan utilizing the four components. Which of Newton's laws is
   being demonstrated in each of the following cases? Write an
   example of the rule we just discussed. Solve this problem, using
   the scientific method.

4. The fourth level, **analysis**, asks students to a) identify the motives,
   reasons, and/or causes for a specific occurrence; b) consider and
   analyze available information to reach a conclusion, inference, or
   generalization based on this information; and, c) analyze a conclusion, inference, or generalization to find evidence to support or
   refute it (Cooper, 1990). Words commonly used for analysis
   questions are *support, analyze, why, determine evidence, identify
   motives or causes, draw conclusions.* Examples: What factors
   influenced the writing of George Orwell? Why was Israel selected
   as the site for the Jewish nation? After studying the French,
   American, and Russian revolutions, what can you conclude about
   the causes of revolution? What information/evidence can you cite
   to support the statement that John Keats was a more effective poet
   than Percy Shelley?

5. The fifth level, **synthesis**, asks students to perform original and
   creative thinking. Words frequently used in synthesis questions

are *predict, produce, write, design, develop, construct, how can we improve.* Examples: Develop a thematic unit on *Space* appropriate for a fourth grade student. What would the United States be like if the South had won the Civil War? How can we measure the height of the building if we can't go into it? Construct an original score of music which would be representative of the Baroque Period. Draw a blueprint of the ideal house for an arctic winter.

6. The sixth level, **evaluation**, requires students to judge the merit of an idea, solution to a problem, or an aesthetic work, or to offer an opinion on an issue. Words frequently used in evaluation questions are *judge, assess, argue, decide, evaluate.* Examples: Which author best exemplifies the characteristic of "Gothic"? Evaluate the effectiveness of the two persuasive essays. Which is the better of the two? Rank the ten essays, with "1" as "most effective" and "10" as "least effective." Which artist do you prefer, Miro or Picasso?

Three inferences that may be drawn from Bloom's Taxonomy are the following:

1. The three higher-level types of questions—analysis, synthesis, and evaluation—have more than one correct answer and take a great deal of time to answer thoroughly.

2. The taxonomy is progressive in nature. Students must have a knowledge base before they can demonstrate comprehension. Students have to make the knowledge their own before they can apply it. In other words, previous levels of the taxonomy must be met before students can be successful in successive ones.

3. Higher level questions take time to construct. Instructors have to plan for high-level questions by constructing them in advance.

Techniques for Asking Questions

1. Distribute attention and questions equitably among males and females. Several studies have indicated that typically instructors direct more questions to males than to females, that males receive more higher-order questions, and that males receive more praise on the quality of their academic work (Sadker and Sadker, 1982).

Most instructors are unaware of this disparate distribution, so the first step is to video a class, to have a colleague observe and report, or to use a self-assessment checklist to record student involvement.

2. Allow students time enough to think and respond. Research shows that the mean amount of time a teacher waits after asking a question is approximately one second (Cooper, 1990). When wait time is increased to three or five seconds, students give longer answers, students ask more questions, student achievement is higher, and students are more willing to volunteer an answer.

3. Address Questions to the Class. To lessen anxiety and to establish a risk-free environment, ask a question to the class, tell them to think individually (allow at least five seconds), tell them to pair with the student sitting beside them and discuss both students' answers, and then to write their response. The instructor can then call on a "pair" to respond.

Responding to Students' Answers

John Goodlad conducted an in-depth observation study of over a thousand classrooms. He concluded that the emotional tone of schools is "flat," neither punitive or joyful perhaps partly attributable in the way teachers deal with student response (Goodlad, 1984).

Neither praise, criticism, nor remediation is the most frequent teacher response. Instructors most often simply *accept* student answers. Accept means that they say "okay" or "uh-huh," or that they do not say anything at all. In Sadker's (1984) research, acceptance occurred in all of the classrooms and it constituted over 50 percent of teacher reactions. There was more acceptance than praise, remediation, and criticism combined. The "okay" classroom is detrimental because students need specific feedback to understand what is expected of them, correct errors, and get help to improve performance.

Techniques for Responding to Students' Questions

1. Actively listen to students' questions. Eye contact, look of interest on instructor's face, and body inclined slightly toward student are all preliminary to answering students' questions if a climate that encourages inquiry is to be promoted.

2. Answer questions clearly and concisely. Many instructors launch into a mini lecture on a broader or related issue instead of simply answering the question. After instructors answer the question, they might say, "Did that answer your question or have I confused, you?" If the instructor is willing to assume the onus of "confuser," students will more likely admit when they have not understood the answer to their questions and a chance once again exists for clarification.

3. Admit not knowing the answer, if that is the case. An occasional honest "I don't know" strengthens the bond of trust between instructor and student, but too many "I don't knows" reduce credibility and eventually respect.

4. Answer with another question. This response helps students clarify and answer their own questions. Another question may break down complex questions into simpler ones that they can answer.

5. Write the question on the board. Many times just writing the question on the board elicits the answer from the student asking the question or from another student in class, especially if the student is a visual learner.

6. Paraphrase the question. The instructor might say "Let me ask the question in a different way" and paraphrase the question.

7. Accept all questions.
   a. If the question does not pertain to issues currently being discussed, "park" it in a circle parking lot drawn on the blackboard. This technique affirms the importance of the student's question but does not break the momentum of the class. It is important to address the question at a more opportune time.
   b. If the question only applies to one or two students in the class, the instructor should say, "That's an important concern to you

but maybe not for everyone else. Could we talk about it immediately after class?"

c. If the question is a thought-provoking, applicable question to the majority of the class, praise the student by saying something such as, "Thanks for asking that important question before I went further. I hadn't thought about that." This response encourages further questions and reassures students they will not be embarrassed or humiliated.

d. If the question is inappropriate or offensive, the instructor might say, "I don't believe that really applies to what we're doing today." Immediately, the instructor's attention should shift to another issue, question, or activity. This lets the student know the instructor considers the question inappropriate, and the student does not receive the desired attention for his efforts. A private conference during office hours may be needed.

In conclusion, instructors must be able to respond to students' questions that promote understanding of the material while maintaining a climate that encourages questions. Responding to questions is an integral component of the classroom structure.

References

Cooper, J. (1990). *Classroom teaching skills*, Boston: Heath and Co.

Dewey, J. (1933). *How we think.* Boston: D. C. Heath.

Gall, M. (1970). The use of questions in teaching. *Review of Educational Research, 40*, 707-721.

Goodlad, J. (1984). *A place called school.* New York: McGraw-Hill, 124.

Sadker, M. and Sadker, D. (1988). *The intellectual exchange: equity and excellence in college teaching.*

Sadker, D. and Sadker, M. (1984). *Promoting effectiveness in classroom instruction, final report*, Contract No. 400-80-0033, Washington, DC: Department of Education.

Sadker, M. and Sadker, D. (1982). *Sex equity handbook for schools.* New York: Longman.

Suggested Reading

Berliner, D. (1984). The half-full glass: A review of research on teaching. In P. Hosford (ed.), *Using What We Know About Teaching.* Alexandria, VA: Association for Supervision and Curriculum Development.

Bonnstetter, R. (1988). Active learning often starts with a question. *Research and Teaching, 18*(2), 95-97.

Bowman, R. (1985). Students know the answers, but what are the questions? *College Teaching 33*, 33-35.

Clarke, J. H.(1988). Designing discussions as group inquiry. *College Teaching, 36*(4), 140-146.

Collins, A.(1988). Different goals of inquiry teaching, *Questioning Exchange, 2*(1), 39-45.

Collins, A.(1982). Goals and strategies of inquiry teaching. In R. Glaser (Ed.), *Advances in Instructional Psychology* . Hillsdale, NJ: Erlbaum.

Collins, A. (1977). Processes in acquiring knowledge. In R. C. Anderson, R. J. Spiro, and W. E. Montague (Eds.), *Schooling and the Acquisition of Knowledge* . Hillsdale, NJ: Erlbaum.

Dillon, J. T. (1983). *Teaching and the art of questioning.* Bloomington, IN: Phi Delta Kappa Educational Foundation.

Ferguson, N. (1986). Encouraging responsibility, active participation, and critical thinking in general psychology students. *Teaching of Psychology 13*, 217-18.

Fuhrmann, B.S. and Grasha, A.F. (1983). *A Practical Handbook for College Teachers.* Boston: Little, Brown.

Gravett, D. (1985). Asking the right questions, a key to good class discussions. *T E T Y C. 12*(4), 300-02.

Holyoak, J. and Koh, K (1987). Surface and structural similarity in analogical transfer. *Memory & Cognition,15*, 332-340.

Kraft, R.(1985). Group-inquiry turns passive students active. *College Teaching, 33*, 149-154.

McKeachie, W., Pintrich, P., Lin, Y., and Smith, D. (1986). *Teaching and learning in the college classroom: A review of the literature.* National Center for Research to Improve Postsecondary Teaching and Learning, University of Michigan.

Myers, L. (1988). Teachers as models of active learning. *College Teaching, 36*, 43-45.

Ortiz, J. (1988, March). *Creating conditions for student questions.* Paper presented at the National Seminar on Successful College Teaching, Orlando

Overholser, J. C. (1988). Clinical utility of the Socratic method. In C. Stout (Ed.), *Annuals of clinical research,* 1-7. Des Plaines, IL: Forest Institute.

Overholser, J. C. (1991). The Socratic method as a technique in psychotherapy supervision. *Professional Psychology: Research and Practice, 22*, 68-74.

Overholser, J. (1992). Socrates in the classroom. *College Teaching, 40*, 14-19.

Palincsar, A., and Brown, A. (1984). Reciprocal teaching of comprehension-fostering and comprehension-monitoring activities. *Cognition and Instruction 1*, 117-75.

Penick, J. E., and Dunkhase, J. A. (1988). Innovations in college science teaching. *Society for College Science Teachers.* Washington, DC

Phoenix, C. (1987). Get them involved!: Styles of high- and low-rated teachers. *College Teaching 35*, 13-15.

Pintrich, P., McKeachie, W., and Lin, Y. (1987). Teaching a course in learning to learn. *Teaching of Psychology 14*, 81-86.

Rocklin, T. (1987). Defining learning: Two classroom activities. *Teaching of Psychology 14*, 228-29.

Seeskin, K. (1987). *Dialogue and discovery: A study in Socratic method.* Albany: SUNY Press.

Seiple, G. (1985). The Socratic method of inquiry. *Dialogue 28*, 16-22.

Sklare, G., Portes, P., and Splete, H. (1985). Developing questioning effectiveness in counseling. *Counselor Education and Supervision 25*, 12-20.

Toppins, A. (1987). Teaching students to teach themselves. *College Teaching 35*, 95-99.

Wilen, W. (1982). *Questioning skills for teachers.* Washington, DC: National Education Association.

Yelon, S. L. and Cooper, C. R. (1984). Discussion: A naturalistic study of a teaching method. *Instructional Science, 13*, 213-224.

Zachry, W. (1985). How I kicked the lecture habit: Inquiry teaching in psychology. *Teaching of Psychology 12*, 129-31.

Establishing A Learning Set

Establishing a learning set is the instructor's ability to clarify, communicate, and arouse interest in learning objectives.

Establishing a learning set has four main purposes; the first is to focus student attention on the lesson. Experience teaches that the first motivational function of the teacher is to engage the student. Next, learning set attempts to create an organizing framework for the ideas, principles, or information that is to follow. Gage and Berliner (1988) relay the importance of advance organizers. They state that "telling students in advance about the way in which a lecture is organized is likely to improve their comprehension and ability to recall and apply what they hear" (p. 405). According to Cooper (1990), a third purpose of learning set is "to extend the understanding and application of abstract ideas through the use of example or analogy. If students are not formal operational thinkers, or abstract thinkers, concepts and principles can be difficult to comprehend. Too, even if students do comprehend the concept or principle, they still may be unable to apply them. These two instances highlight the importance of examples or analogies in ensuring comprehension. The fourth purpose of establishing a learning set is to stimulate interest, enthusiasm, and participation in a lesson. Active involvement is a powerful motivational tool.

Often, learning set preparation consists of distributing a syllabus, telling the class about the upcoming class, or asking students to read the next chapter. In and of themselves, these activities do not arouse student interest, nor do they help students activate prior learning or help them to organize and remember subsequent learning. Planning and preparation, then, are the keys to establishing a learning set.

Learning Set Activities

1. *Learning Objectives.* Before any thought can be given to learning set activities, instructors must define specifically what it is they want their students to know or be able to do at the end of a semester, a unit, and a class. All three must be considered for maximum effectiveness. Once objectives have been established for a semester, then objectives may be established for units (which are usually blocks of testable material), and then, finally, objectives can be established for each class period. Learning objectives provide instructors and students with a benchmark against which they can see where they are going, measure their own progress toward that end, and then determine their degree of successful completion. Objectives clearly stated in the syllabus and class objectives on the board or overhead at the beginning of each class period will accomplish that end.

2. *Overviews.* Once objectives have been shared, an overview could be given. An overview is simply a summary of what is to be accomplished. It introduces students to new material by emphasizing the key concepts, principles, terminology, and general structure of the material. Most instructors do this automatically, but with preparation, variations of an overview may be presented.

   a. **Outline.** An outline of the lesson could be placed on an overhead to convey ideas readily and precisely in order to prepare students for what is to come.

   b. **Pictures.** Most students find a pictorial overview appealing. A picture which introduces the lesson on the Battle of Gettysburg, a lesson on Renaissance architecture, a lesson on Faulkner's South motivates and entices even the most unmotivated student. The problem is, of course, finding the right picture. Planning early and alerting your librarian of your needs can often produce miraculous results!

   c. **Trigger Films.** A 10- to 15-minute piece of film may capture students' attention and stimulate discussion on an upcoming chapter or unit. For instance, what better way to introduce the persuasive speech in Public Speaking than to show a persuasive speech and then to "vote" on its effectiveness. A discussion of its characteristics could follow. At the end of the unit, the class could repeat the entire procedure. Certainly, this would be an ideal way to determine mastery of the material.

d. **Interviews.** One way to introduce a unit is to have students go through the text, turning headings into questions and "interviewing" the teacher. Students are actively involved, the teacher has the opportunity to imply importance of ideas by the depth of answer provided to the question, and the class gets an overview in a unique way.

3. *Pretests.* A pretest is any set of related questions given to students before instruction to determine what students already know of the material to be taught. A pretest can be an important set induction, for the student pays attention to the word *test* and as a result, notices the content of issues, problems, and questions, for they rightly assume they will see similar items again on a posttest! Pretests usually take the form of an objective written test; however, oral exercises, interviews, and performance tasks may suffice as well.

a. **Response Cards.** For an oral pretest, have each student fold a sheet of paper lengthwise with a big "T" written on one side and a big "F" on the other. The instructor asks true or false questions to determine prior knowledge. Students respond by holding up the appropriate side of the paper.

b. **Performance Tasks.** The instructor can assign a task to determine what students already know about content and process. For example, an English instructor could assign a comparison/contrast essay before instruction on same, or a biology teacher might assign an experiment to observe the process of tackling the problem, or a geography teacher might ask students to fill in a blank map of Europe before actual instruction.

4. *Advance Organizers.* Advance organizers provide a conceptual framework that students can use to clarify the process. Instead of concentrating so heavily on content as do pretests and overviews, advance organizers emphasize context. Typically, an advance organizer is prose in form; however, the pictorial organizer is

gaining popularity as instructors address different learning styles. One of the more popular advance organizers is the concept map.

   a. **Concept Map.** A concept map is essentially a pictorial outline. For example, if the skeletal system were the unit of study, the instructor might show the five main subordinate topics—bone tissue, bone organs, fracture healing, osteogenesis, and calcium homeostasis—under the main heading of "Skeletal System." By distributing this "whole picture" concept map to the student, the instructor establishes a learning set. This type of visual aid "takes advantage of the extraordinary human capacity for visual memory" (Cliburn, 1990) and caters to the visual learning style of so many students. As a follow up, students could produce concept maps of the five subordinate topics as the unit or discussion progressed. Cliburn (1990) conducted a study to evaluate the effects of concept maps on learning and retention. He presented a three-week skeletal system unit to both his control group and experimental group, using the same lectures and text, but the control group used no concept maps. The immediate posttest and delayed posttest scores of students in the experimental group suggested significantly better learning and retention.

   b. **Comparative Concept Maps.** Cliburn (1990) also advocates the use of comparative concept maps which serve to link two things for a pictorial comparison. This map serves to integrate knowledge, which is essential for critical thinking but is often difficult or impossible for students to do on their own if they are concrete thinkers who have not reached the capability for abstract thought.

Other Learning Set Tactics

1. *Role Play.* To introduce behavioral modification, B. F. Skinner could make an "appearance" in the guise of a student, the instructor, or an outside speaker to explain his theory.

2. *What I Know for Sure and What I Think I Know.* This exercise is an excellent way to generate student interest and involvement, and, at the same time, assess students' prior knowledge. It is very

simple. The teacher introduces a new concept by making two columns on the board and titling one "What I Know for Sure" and the other "What I Think I Know." The teacher then calls upon someone to add one item to either column, depending on the issue or concept. For example, classical conditioning, Somalia, Bill of Rights, Figurative Language, Skeletal System, Martin Luther King, Jr., could all be appropriate starting points. The list is literally infinite. After each student has voiced an item for the board and each student has copied the entire chart, research into the correctness of the chart may begin. As discussion, research, or reading continues, the chart is modified to correct inaccuracies or to add new information.

3. *Analogy.* Students are more likely to be motivated to learn if the instructional objectives are related to current events or interests. The instructor might ask a history class to list ways that the Bosnia or Rwanda civil wars are like the U. S. Civil War or an American history instructor might ask a class to list the similarities of Grover Cleveland's and Bill Clinton's personal ethics. Today's music, art, literature, politics are indeed similar to previous periods in history; thus, it is important to note the similarities so that students understand that they are not just studying theories, ideas, or concepts that are far removed from their lives today. Relevancy motivates students, and as such, establishes a learning set.

4. *Case Study.* Case studies are a general vehicle for concept instruction. The instructor could introduce the case study and set the scene and encourage discussion of the case. After instruction, the students could solve the case using their newfound knowledge.

Establishing a learning set is one of the most important teacher behaviors because how students approach instructional objectives will determine the time and energy they invest in learning. Because students' ability levels, learning styles, and interest levels are so diverse, this behavior is quite demanding of the instructor. Effective demonstration of this skill requires planning, time, creativity, and the willingness to try many and varied methods.

References

Cliburn, J. (1990, February). Concept maps to promote meaningful learning, *JCST*, 212-216.

Cooper, J. (1990). *Classroom Teaching Skills*. Boston: D. C. Heath and Co., 167-180.

Gage, N. and Berliner, D. (1988). *Educational Psychology*. Boston: Houghton-Mifflin.

Suggested Reading

Alvarez, M. C., and Risko, V. J. (1985). The effects of thematic organizers on comprehension and learning. In G. H. McNineh (Ed.), *Reading research in 1984: Comprehension, computers, communication*, 35-37. Athens, GA: American Reading Forum.

Anderson, R. C., and Pearson, P. D. (1984). A schema-theoretic view of basic processes in reading comprehension. In P. D. Pearson (Ed.), *Handbook of Reading Research*, 255-291. New York: Longman.

Arnaudin, M.W., Mintzes, J.J., Dunn, C.S., and Shafer, T.S. (1984). Concept mapping in college science teaching. *Journal of College Science Teaching 14*(2), 117-21.

Ault, C.R. (1985).Concept mapping as a study strategy in earth science. *Journal of College Science Teaching 15*(1), 38-44.

Berliner, D.C., and Rosenshine, B.V. (Eds.).(1988). *Talks to Teacher*. New York: Random House.

Bloom, B. S. (1985). *Developing talent in young people*. New York: Ballentine.

Breen, E. J. (1982). A study of the influence of previewing techniques on the reading comprehension of community college students. *Dissertation Abstracts International*, (Doctoral dissertation, University of Washington), 43(12), 3819A.

Brooks, L. W., and Dansereau, D. F. (1983). Effects of structural schema training and text organization on expository prose processing. *Journal of Educational Psychology*, 75, 811-820.

Cliburn, J. W., and Cotten, D.R. (1986). *Concept maps as advance organizers: Effects on learning and retention in a college anatomy and physiology course*. Unpublished manuscript, University of Southern Mississippi.

Cliburn, J. W. (1986). Using concept maps to sequence instructional materials. *Journal of College Science Teaching 15*(4), 377-79.

Cliburn, J. W. (1985). *An ausubelian approach to instruction: The use of concept maps as advance organizers in a junior college anatomy and physiology course*. (Doctoral thesis, University of Southern Mississippi).

Cliburn, J.W. (1985). Using concept maps as advance organizers in a college biology course. *Journal of the Mississippi Academy of Sciences ,30*,78.

Cohen, R. (1983). Self-generated questions as an aid to reading comprehension. *The Reading Teacher, 36* (3), 770-775.

Dick, W., and Carey, L. (1985). *The Systematic Design of Instruction*. Glenview: Scott Foresman and Company.

Dunkin, M. J. (Ed.).(1987). *International Encyclopedia of Teaching and Teacher Education.* Oxford: Pergamon Press.

Gage, N. L., and Berliner, D.C. (1988). *Educational Psychology.* Boston: Houghton Mifflin Company .

Greene, B. (1990). Using study guides. *Reading Psychology, 2*(1), 75-82.

Magnen, B. (1989). *147 Practical Tips for Teaching Professors. Madison,* WI: Magna Publications.

Malone, J., and Dekkers, J. (1984). The concept map as an aid to instruction in science and mathematics. *School Science and Mathematics 84,* 220-31.

McEneany, J. (1990). Do advance organizers facilitate learning? A review of subsumption theory. *Journal of Research and Development, 23*(2), 89-96.

Novak, J. D., and Gowin, D.B. (1984). *Learning How to Learn.* New York: Cambridge University Press.

Ost, D.H. (1987). The evolution of a biology curriculum. *The American Biology Teacher 49,* 153-156.

Sulzer-Azaroff, B., and Mayer, G.R.(1986). *Achieving Educational Excellence.* New York: Holt, Rinehart and Winston.

Swafford, J. (1990, Fall/Winter). Comprehensive strategies research and college developmental studies students. *Forum for Reading,* 6-14.

Swafford, J., and Alvermann, D. E. (1989). Postsecondary research base for content reading strategies. *Journal of Reading, 33,* 164-169.

Swafford, J., and Hague, S. A. (1987, October). *Content area reading strategies: Myth or reality.* Paper presented at the 31st Annual College Reading Association Conference, Baltimore, Maryland.

Thistlethwaite, L. L. (1983). Effects of using text structure and self-generated questions on comprehension of information from three levels of text structure as measured by free recall. (Doctoral dissertation, University of Missouri-Columbia). *Dissertation Abstracts International, 45*(2), 480A. (University Microfilms No. DA8412816).

Tierney, R., and Cunningham, J. (1984). Research on teaching reading comprehension. In P. D. Pearson (Ed.), *Handbook of Reading Research .* New York: Longman. 609-655.

Wittrock, M. C. (Ed.).(1986). *Handbook of Research on Teaching,* (3rd ed.). New York: Macmillan.

Creativity

Creativity is vital to an individual's quality of life and contribution to society. Complex problem-solving demands individuals who are skilled in critical and creative thought. The development of creative capacity increases fluency and flexibility of thought, curiosity, open-mindedness, and sense of adventure (Davis, 1983). These traits are certainly desirable of students in our classes and will serve them well outside the classroom. However, there are several blocks to the recognition and development of creative thought in the classroom. Among these are (1) concerns for clear definitions; (2) concerns related to methodology and implementation; and, (3) concerns related to assessment of creativity.

Definitions

There is a wide disparity in defining and understanding concepts of creativity, its processes, and its products or outcomes. We understand active, thinking classes to be characterized by students who are involved in the generation and recombination of ideas, processes, and products to solve real and theoretical problems. In light of this, it becomes apparent that creative and critical thinking are interrelated functions which must be developed and used in conjunction with each other. Each contains components of both convergent thought (that which unites or pulls ideas together) and divergent thought (the generation of ideas without regard to relationships or similarities), though the latter is often emphasized in creativity (Davis, 1983).

Divergent and Convergent Processes in Creativity

Fact Finding

Divergent: listing of facts or facets of the problem
Convergent: narrowing of this list to a specific definition of the problem

Idea Finding

Divergent: brainstorming for possibilities and alternatives

Solution Finding

Divergent: lists criteria for evaluation
Convergent: selects most important criteria

Imagination is not simply a free-fall of ideas but a direction of ideas toward that perceived ultimate "future state." Analytical thought is highly involved in describing the problem and analyzing connections between what is known and unknown (Grossman and Wiseman, 1993). Thus, critical and creative thought are limited in both scope and usefulness when separated from each other. That is, until an idea, issue, or problem is generated, critical thinking skills cannot be put to productive use. On the other hand, creative thought can generate ideas but relies on critical processes to distinguish between appropriate and inappropriate ones. Though this work and other sources often discuss creativity and critical thinking in separate terms and with differing strategies for implementation, the overlap is quite strong. We can confidently create an active learning environment where both creative and critical thought is active. That is, we need not create artificial assessments in which one aspect of thought is emphasized at the exclusion of the other as this is not the nature of thought.

Thus, contrary to popular definition, creativity is not a product but encompasses certain thinking processes, actions and outcomes. Furthermore, creativity is not a gift bestowed on certain individuals and unavailable to others. Rather, persons who have learned to value creativity and desire to develop their creative potential are more likely to direct conscious effort toward trying to produce things that are original and appropriate and are recognized by others for their creative products. Leland (1990) affirms that every human being is born with creative powers and the ability to use them in some way. She states that creativity is not a magical ingredient of personality but rather an attitude one holds about opportunities for choices. It appears, then, that the responsibility of educators is to provide everyone with an environment that values and rewards creativity and the opportunities to engage in creative work.

A more formal definition defines creativity as:

> the process of becoming sensitive to or aware of problems, deficiencies, and gaps in knowledge, where there is no learned solution; bringing together existing information from memory or external resources; defining the difficulty or identifying the missing elements; searching for solutions; making guesses and producing alternatives to solve problems; testing and retesting alternatives; perfecting them; and communicating the results (Torrance, 1978).

Methodology and Implementation

While in many cases specific courses and programs have been developed for facilitating the development of creativity, many would argue that the most practical approach involves the inclusion of opportunities for creativity within the content of normal classwork. Problems that have meaning and purpose to the people attempting to solve them will engage those people in serious thought (Rickler, 1989). This presents a need for domain-specific, concrete teaching methodologies.

If knowledge is presented to students as a determined set of data rather than as a product of a creative effort to accomplish a goal, students are robbed of opportunities to reason, reflect, redefine, and refine knowledge for themselves, becoming passive and conforming learners (Stewart, 1988). The dilemma is that students in schools are asked to react, possibly even critically, to what is put before them, but outside school, life requires them to actively create plans and to take actions and initiatives (de Bono, 1986). As instructors, we are not purposely limiting creative thought, but emphasis upon content coverage, right answers, conformity and success inhibits student exploration and experimentation where the probability of success is risked (Bozik, 1990). Lyman (1989) lists several risks that often block students' willingness to engage in creative endeavors: need to define one's goals, fear of failure (most pronounced in individuals with low self esteem), fear of success (risk of surpassing one's peers), too much security to risk the unknown, and fear of change. Instructors who wish to support the development of creativity must provide place in the classroom for intuition, invention, and innovation, all of which are much riskier behaviors than those students have become accustomed to in traditional modes of teaching, learning, and assessment.

To practice creativity in the classroom, students must be provided with the opportunity to engage in four processes often defined as stages of the creative process:

1. *Preparation* - opportunities to look at a problem from multiple perspectives without judgment of their usefulness or validity. Students are engaged in loosening rigid patterns of thinking and provoking new possibilities. The more ideas generated, the more choices there will be and the more likely an appropriate one will emerge. Brainstorming techniques have been demonstrated to aid this process (see Classroom Discussion).

2. *Incubation* - an unforced surfacing of thoughts and ideas which begin to define and identify the problem for the individual. This involves the ability of the individual to make shifts in thinking from one concept to another and to embellish or add detail to create a more comprehensive image.

3. *Illumination* - the sudden appearance of ideas and solutions as one continues to ponder the problem in an environment free of an probability to produce. This stage, often referred to as the "Ah!," is most successful when pressure is not applied to produce a product, now!

4. *Verification* - critical evaluation and revision of original solutions.

It is important to note that originality is not necessarily mandetory. It has been said that creativity is more "repatterning existing material rather than manufacturing it" (Hawley and Hawley, 1975).

Grossman and Wiseman (1993) recommend that creative opportunities are offered before a formal presentation of facts. While it is necessary that before initiating the creative process the problem solver has already reviewed data relevant to solving the problem, extensive focus on the facts initially means that mental judgments are more likely to be based on initial perceptions. An attitude shift essential to the generation of new ideas may be more difficult or impossible due to this initial bias. Creativity must be able to focus on what could be rather than what is.

Activities and Assignments

1. Frequently use assignments that call for divergent thought. Brent and Felder (1992) offer these specific suggestions:

   List three ways (ten ways, as many ways as you can think of) to evaluate economic profitability (measure the viscosity of a fluid, deal with a disruptive student in a class, injure yourself when running the next experiment in this lab).

   Suppose we build the bridge (perform the test, run the experiment, apply the treatment, teach the lesson) the way our theoretical calculation indicated we should, and the result we get is not at all what we predicted. List as many possible explanations as you can for the unexpected findings. Then prioritize the list in order of decreasing likelihood and indicate how you might go about tracking down the real cause.

2. Designate a portion of the points or grade allotted to an assignment for creative approaches. Students have been known to enhance projects with self-designed pamphlets, games, videos, models, demonstrations, etc.

3. A highly creative form of role play called roletaking is described by Gallo (1989). Roletaking is a small group role play, without an audience, involving empathetic role play from multiple perspectives followed by evaluative reflection on the experience. It begins with a presented or learner-generated issue or problem. Each participant adopts a role which, when enacted, provides definition and detail of the problem which leads to resolution. Roles are rotated among participants or new roles are generated and enacted.

Each participant works through the issue from at least three contrasting perspectives. This occurs within several concurrent groups. Following the period of roletaking, participants engage in a reflective, evaluative discussion in which the issue is defined and detailed from the viewpoints generated. Resolutions and their multiple consequences are evaluated. Gallo believes that regular practice of roletaking fosters increased participant tolerance for complexity, ambiguity, and deferred judgment indicative of creative thinking. She also proposes that it produces a new organization of information, a new or variant knowledge structure comprised from both cognitive and feeling processes. It fosters imagination by providing opportunities for immersive, holistic, spontaneous, and novel responses to problems that are engaging and complex and intrinsically motivating.

4. Challenge students to find analogies or metaphors to describe concepts or issues in course content. This task of describing relationships and multiple connections fosters insight into new perspectives on old problems and allows known information to be presented in a discovery mode (Grossman and Wiseman, 1993). In fact, the use of metaphors, figures of speech, examples, stories, anecdotes, word pictures, quotations and slogans in the classroom stirs students to search for creative representation of knowledge (Litterst and Eyo, 1993).

5. Provide time for class discussion in which the direction of the discussion grows out of the participation of the students. Be attentive to exploiting opportunities for imagination as they occur. (See Class Discussion for specific discussion techniques.)

6. Littert and Eyo (1993) advocate the use of fuzzy assignments that lack set criteria and the normal definitions that lock students in rote compliance with teacher expectations. Tell students that they have been empowered to do as they wish, that there is not a single "right" way to do the assignment and they should let their imaginations run wild. They recommend dodging the questions that signify mental locks, i.e., How many pages?; Do I need visual aids?; What do you want?; etc. However, after allowing for a period of creative tension, providing direction can aid learning. Unbridled imagination can breed frustration.

7. Discuss creativity openly with students. Verbally create a climate that values imagination. Accept a variety of student responses, refrain from offering opinions and value judgments.

8. Exhibit open responses to student input. An open response requires students to continue and expand their thoughts and to think for themselves. Closed responses, even if praise, can bring closure to students' thought processes. Open responses might recognize the student's contribution and ask the student to further describe, select, analyze, compare, contrast, distinguish, categorize, explain, evaluate, generalize, hypothesize, predict, etc. (Thacker, 1990).

9. Sternberg and Lubart (1991) favor fewer long-term assignments and projects over several short-term. This provides students with the opportunity to invest much personal effort. These are most likely to be successful if students have had some voice in the selection of their assignment and therefore have some intrinsic motivation. Long-term assignments require students to define their problems, structure the problems, make connections, and pose new problems as well as reach solutions. Sternberg and Lubart also recommend that such assignments be designed to involve students in acquiring knowledge in the same context it is normally used; that is, in a way that makes it clear to them why the information they are learning is important. Students also have a greater opportunity to develop a tolerance for ambiguity. Creativity is often stifled in short-term assignments because ambiguities must be solved quickly. Lacking time to mull over a problem, they select a more obvious, though less creative, approach.

10. Student journals provide an ongoing forum for creative thought and expression. Hols (1990) asks students to select a topic or theme according to their own interests and pursue the development of this theme in the journal throughout the semester. Students decide what to include in their journals based on information they gather in newspapers, news magazines, radio and television newscasts, books, scholarly publications, government documents, films, lectures, public events, personal contacts, etc. To encourage creativity, these entries are not to summarize or report but rather offer the student's own comments, criticisms, analyses, and con-

clusions. They are encouraged to define a central problem to the theme and to focus more on this central issue as the semester progresses.

11. Assign students to represent a theme, style, or interpretation of a written work in a medium other than writing. Students may draw, paint, sculpt, build, videotape, use music, story telling, comedy, pantomime, etc., to convey their ideas (Reed, 1990).

Assessment of Creativity

To encourage students to take creative approaches to class work, we must control the degree of risk in assessment. Sternberg and Lubart (1991) explain how risk stifles creativity.

> Risking an unusual response on an exam or an idiosyncratic approach in a paper is a step likely to be taken only with great trepidation, because of the fear that a low or failing grade on a specific assignment may ruin one's chances for a good grade in the course. Moreover, there is usually some safe response that is at least good enough to earn the grade for which one is aiming.

In the evaluation of creative work, the instructor initially reads all of the student writing or views all of the student work without judgment. Rather, the instructor asks questions and makes comments that invite students to revise their writing or other work—and thus their thinking—to go further than they went in their initial work.

Traditional assessment has often been guilty of rewarding students for repeating answers rather than challenging conclusions. Several scholars have reported that external evaluation or the expectation of it is not conducive to creative learning. Some have even advocated entirely abolishing grades. Wilcox (1988) recommends modifying grading practices. Students should be rewarded for demonstrating how they can use facts they learn to find and solve problems, carry out processes and connect ideas.

Classroom Environment Conducive to Creativity

The creative classroom will be characterized by several key criteria (Wilcox, 1988):

1. *Teacher modeling of good thinking behaviors.* Such instructors demonstrate excitement and enthusiasm for challenges and complex tasks that require new thought. These view instructions as engaging in the discovery of knowledge rather than the reporting of that already known.
2. *Teacher-student and student-student interaction* is emphasized so that the amount of information given to students is significantly reduced, letting students discover it on their own through interactive approaches.
3. *A development of student autonomy occurs.* Teachers are increasingly perceived as resources rather than external, authoritative repositories of knowledge.

Students who have not yet developed creative skill look for certainty and are intolerant of ambiguity. They often give up prematurely or exhibit impulsiveness and overconfidence in their ideas. They ignore evidence that does not support their favored possibility and refuse to modify their thinking when necessary. Creative thinkers develop self autonomy, initiating and monitoring their own thinking. They are tolerant and appreciative of ambiguity and complexity, searching for contradictory evidence to challenge previously held possibilities. It is not difficult to see which is desirable in our classrooms, nor is it difficult to recognize the immense challenge in leading students "to the water" and getting them to "drink."

The creative classroom is likely to have a very different orientation than that to which we may have grown accustomed. As teachers, we have often claimed full responsibility for the success of the class. Students, then, having no part in the creation of the class, have no strong feelings for its success, as long as they can figure out what is expected of them and perform up to expectations for a desired grade (Elliott, 1989). The creative classroom is purposely open enough to allow students to make their own decisions, define and solve emerging problems, practice inquiry, discover their own purposes for writing, develop their own organization patterns, and become more secure and confident observers, readers, writers, and thinkers (Wolfe, 1989).

References

Bozik, M. (1990). Teachers as creative decision makers: Implications for curriculum. *Action in Teacher Education, 12*(1), 50-54.

Brent, R., and Felder, R.M. (1992). Writing assignments - pathways to corrections, clarity, creativity. *College Teaching, 40*(2), 43-47.

Davis, G. (1983). *Creativity is Forever.* Dubuque, IA: Kendall-Hunt Publishing Company.

de Bono, E. (1986). Beyond critical thinking. *Curriculum Review, 25*(3), 12-16.

Elliott, M. (1989). There's no such thing as too many cooks in the classroom. *Innovation Abstracts, 12*(25).

Evans, M.G. (1995). Teaching behaviors, assessment, and other factors that influence development of student and faculty creativity in Kentucky Community Colleges. Thesis proposal for Southern Illinois University, Carbondale, IL.

Gallo, D. (1989). Educating for empathy, reason and imagination. *Journal of Creative Behavior, 23*(2), 98-115.

Grossman, S.R., and Wiseman, E.E. (1993). Seen operating principles for enhanced creative problem solving training. *Journal of Creative Behavior, 27*(1), 1-17.

Hawley, R., and Hawley, I. (1975). *Developing Human Potential.* Amherst, MA: Educational Research Associates Press.

Hols, W. (1990). A versatile and fun learning experience: The student journal. *Innovation Abstracts, 12*(24).

Leland, N. (1990). *The Creative Artist.* Cincinnati, OH: North Light Books.

Ligekis, C. (1989). Teaching learning project - fun for student and educator. *Innovation Abstracts, 12*(6).

Litterst, J. K., and Eyo, B.A. (1993). Developing classroom imagination: Shaping and energizing a suitable climate for growth, discovery, and vision. *Journal of Creative Behavior, 27*(4), 270-282.

Lyman, D.H. (1989). Being creative. *Training and Development Journal, 43*, 44-50.

Reed, R. (1990). Promoting creativity for student-direct learning. *Innovation Abstracts, 12*(3).

Rockler, M. J. (1989). Teaching thinking skills for the twenty-first century. Paper presented at the Annual Meeting of the Association of Teacher Educators, St. Louis, MO. ERIC Reproduction Service No. 304440.

Sternberg, R.J., and Lubart, T. I. (1991). Creating creative minds. *Phi Delta Kappan, 72*(8), 608-614.

Stewart, W. J. (1988). Stimulating intuitive thinking through problem solving. *The Clearing House, 62*, 175-176.

Thacker, J. (1990). Critical and creative thinking in the classroom. *ERS Spectrum, 8*(4), 28-31.

Torrance, E. P. (1978). Healing qualities of creative behavior. *Creative Child and Adult Quarterly, 3*(3), 146-58.

Wilcox, R. T. (1988). Teaching thinking while exploring educational controversies. *The Clearing House,* 62,161-164.

Wolfe, D. (1989). In defense of vague assignments. *The Clearing House,* 62, 100-201.

Suggested Reading

Aronowitz, B. (1986). Keeping the postman busy: Reestablishing the group in a weekend college class. *Innovation Abstracts, 8*(2).

Barber, L., and others (1990). Building community through research projects. *Innovation Abstracts, 12*(25).

Black, J. A. (1990). Explanation games: If he'd seen the sawdust. *Innovation Abstracts, 12*(21).

Chance, P. (1986). *Thinking in the Classroom: A survey of programs.* New York: Teachers College Press.

Emig, J. (1983). *The Web of Meaning.* Upper Montclair, NJ: Boynton/Cook.

Ghislen, B. (1955). *The Creative Process.* New York: New American Library.

Gowan, J. C., Khateno, J., and Torrance, E.P. (1981). *Creativity: It's Educational Implications,* (2nd ed.). Kendall-Hunt Publishing Company, Dubuque, IA.

Paoni, F. (1990). I know it when I see it: Great teaching. *Innovation Abstracts, 12*(23).

Piwetz, E. (1989). Survival strategies for nursing students. *Innovation Abstracts, 11*(12).

Reid, R.K. (1994). Creative thinking exercise. *The American Biology Teacher,* 56(4), 226-228.

Roweton, W.E. (1989). Enhancing individual creativity in American business and education. *Journal of Creative Behavior,* 23(4), 248-257.

Schon, D. A. (1987). *Educating the Reflective Practitioner: Toward a New Design for Teaching and Learning in the Professions.* San Francisco: Jossey-Bass.

Shallcross, D.J., and Gawienowski, A. M. (1989). Top experts address issues of creativity gap in higher education. *Journal of Creative Behavior,* 23(2), 75-84.

Svinicki, M. (1990, Summer). Changing the face of your teaching. *New Directions for Teaching and Learning,* 42.

Torrance, E. P. (1992). A national climate for creativity and invention. *Gifted Child Today,* 15(1), 10-14.

Walters, B. (1990). The algebra cup. *Innovation Abstracts, 12*(14).

Will, G. (1989). O robin! My captain! *Innovation Abstracts, 20*(24).

Wood, J., and Vick, F. (1990). A story of collaborative publishing. *Innovation Abstracts, 12*(16).

Closure

Anyone who watches weekly television shows understands the meaning and importance of *closure*. Script writers use closure when they bring the show to a satisfying close—that is, all the loose ends have been tied up, the conflict has been resolved, and the main characters are at peace. Teachers use closure in much the same way—to help students bring things together in their own minds and to make sense out of what has been going on during the presentation or activity.

Closure is the instructor's ability to wrap things up before moving into a new topic or activity or the ability to tie things together at the end of class. Its use is important because it leaves students feeling comfortable and satisfied, but its use is imperative because research into the psychology of learning indicates that learning increases when teachers make a conscious effort to help students organize the information presented to them (Gage and Berliner, 1988, p. 405).

Closure performs three functions. During class, closure draws attention to the end of a lesson segment. It is important, then, to cue students to the fact that they have reached an important part in the presentation. A second major function of closure is to help organize student learning. A great deal of information and many activities may have been covered, and it is the teacher's responsibility to show students how it all fits together into a meaningful whole. Finally, closure reinforces the major points to be learned.

Examples of When to Use Closure (Cooper, 1990, p. 99)

1. To end a long unit
2. To consolidate learning of a new concept or principle
3. To close a discussion

4. To end a skill-building activity
5. To follow up a film, tape, television program
6. To close a question-and-answer session
7. To consolidate learning experiences on a field trip
8. To reinforce the presentation of a guest speaker
9. To follow up a homework assignment
10. To end a lab exercise
11. To organize thinking around a new concept or principle

Examples of Scenarios

1. The teacher wishes to call students' attention to the fact that the first of three concepts is ready for closure. Teacher closure: "Before moving on to the second important concept, let's review the main points of the first concept." The teacher then reviews the major points using a prepared outline or one developed on the board during the lesson.

   This closure uses a verbal cue to draw attention to the end of the first concept—"before moving on to the second important concept." It reviews the major points, and it organizes student thinking by using an outline.

2. The teacher has been facilitating a discussion, and the time has come to bring it to a close. Teacher closure: "Sandra, would you please summarize what has been said thus far and point out what you felt were the major points covered?" This closure indicates that the teacher is bringing an end to the discussion by requesting a student summary. It summarizes what students have been discussing, and it helps students organize their ideas by asking students to list major points (Cooper, 1990, p. 101).

   Closure activities are many and varied depending on individual students in individual classes. The following activities may need to be modified depending on an instructor's specific needs.

1. *Minutes*—Boris (1983) suggests that a student be assigned each day to keep the "minutes" of the day's discussion and that each class period begin with a reading of the minutes.

2. *Three-minute summaries*—students spend three minutes writing a summary of main points in their journals or learning logs. One

student is called on to share and the teacher takes this opportunity to correct misinformation or to add to the student's summary.

3. *Skeletal outlines*—Place a skeletal outline on the overhead. At appropriate closing points, have students fill in outline.

4. *Case studies*—Using a case at the end of a unit is one way to assess student ability to solve problems using knowledge, concepts, and/or skills just learned. Cases provide an opportunity to apply course content as well as to provide a closure for a long unit.

5. *Practice test questions*—At the end of a class segment or an entire class, students could construct two possible test questions based upon the information presented thus far. This activity could double for closure as well as for a way for the instructor to assess formatively and correct any misinformation. If the instructor actually used some of those student-generated test questions on the future test, students would be motivated to take this activity quite seriously!

6. *Objectives*—If the day's objectives are listed on the board, have a student check off the objective as accomplished and summarize. Assuming the instructor has at least three or four objectives for the class period, this is a way to involve more students in the closure and to ensure that each class segment is "tied up" before moving on to the next objective.

7. *Think Pair/Share*—have students individually brainstorm for 1 minute on the most important points from a segment or a lesson. Call out "pair/share"; students will pair and share individual major points until a consensus can be reached in order to share with the rest of the class. The teacher lists on the blackboard the results of each pair.

8. *Quiz*—the teacher prepares a 5- to 10-question quiz on information just presented. The students each fold a piece of paper lengthwise with a big colored "T" on one side and an "F" on the other. The teacher orally administers the quiz while the students answer by holding up the appropriate answer—"T" for True or "F" for False.

9. *Application*—The teacher can ask students an application problem of material just learned to double as closure as well as formative assessment.

References

Berliner, D. and Gage, N. (1988). *Educational Psychology*. Boston: Houghton Mifflin Co.

Boris, E. Z. (1983). Classroom minutes: A valuable teaching device. *Improving College and University Teaching, 31*(2), 70-73.

Cooper, J. (1990). *Classroom Teaching Skills*. Boston: D. C. Heath and Co.

Suggested Reading

Berliner, D. C., and Rosenshine, B.V. (Eds.).(1988). *Talks to Teachers*. New York: Random House.

Bloom, B. S. (1985).*Developing Talent in Young People*. New York: Ballentine.

Dick, W., and Carey, L (1985). *The Systematic Design of Instruction*. Glenview: Scott Foresman and Company.

Dunkin, M. J. (Ed.).(1987). *International Encyclopedia of Teaching and Teacher Education*. Oxford: Pergamon Press.

Gage, N. L., and Berliner, D.C. (1988). *Educational Psychology*. Boston: Houghton Mifflin Company.

Sulzer-Azaroff, B., and Mayer, G.R. (1986). *Achieving Educational Excellence*. New York: Holt, Rinehart and Winston.

Wittrock, M. C. (Ed.).(1986). *Handbook of Research on Teaching*, (3rd ed.). New York: Macmillan.